I0816111

ROUTE 66

The First 100 Years

Jim Ross and Shellee Graham

Reedy Press
PO Box 5131
St. Louis, MO 63139, USA
www.reedypress.com

Library of Congress Control Number: 2024948756

ISBN: 9781681065823

Design by Eric Marquard and Jill Halpin

Front Cover Photos:
Road Shot: Jim Ross; *Bridge Photo:* Arizona Historical Society; *General Store Gas Pumps:* Jim Ross
Snow Cap: Tim Anderson; *66 Motel:* Anthony Reichardt

Back Cover Photos:
Dinosaur: Jim Ross; *Rattlesnakes Billboard:* 66postcards.com; *Indian Chief:* Jeff Jensen

Printed in Canada
26 27 28 29 5 4 3

Dedication

In memory of Cyrus Stevens Avery, father of the Mother Road.
(1871–1963)

Essie, Leighton, Gordon, and Cyrus Avery.
The State Historical Society of Missouri Photograph Collection

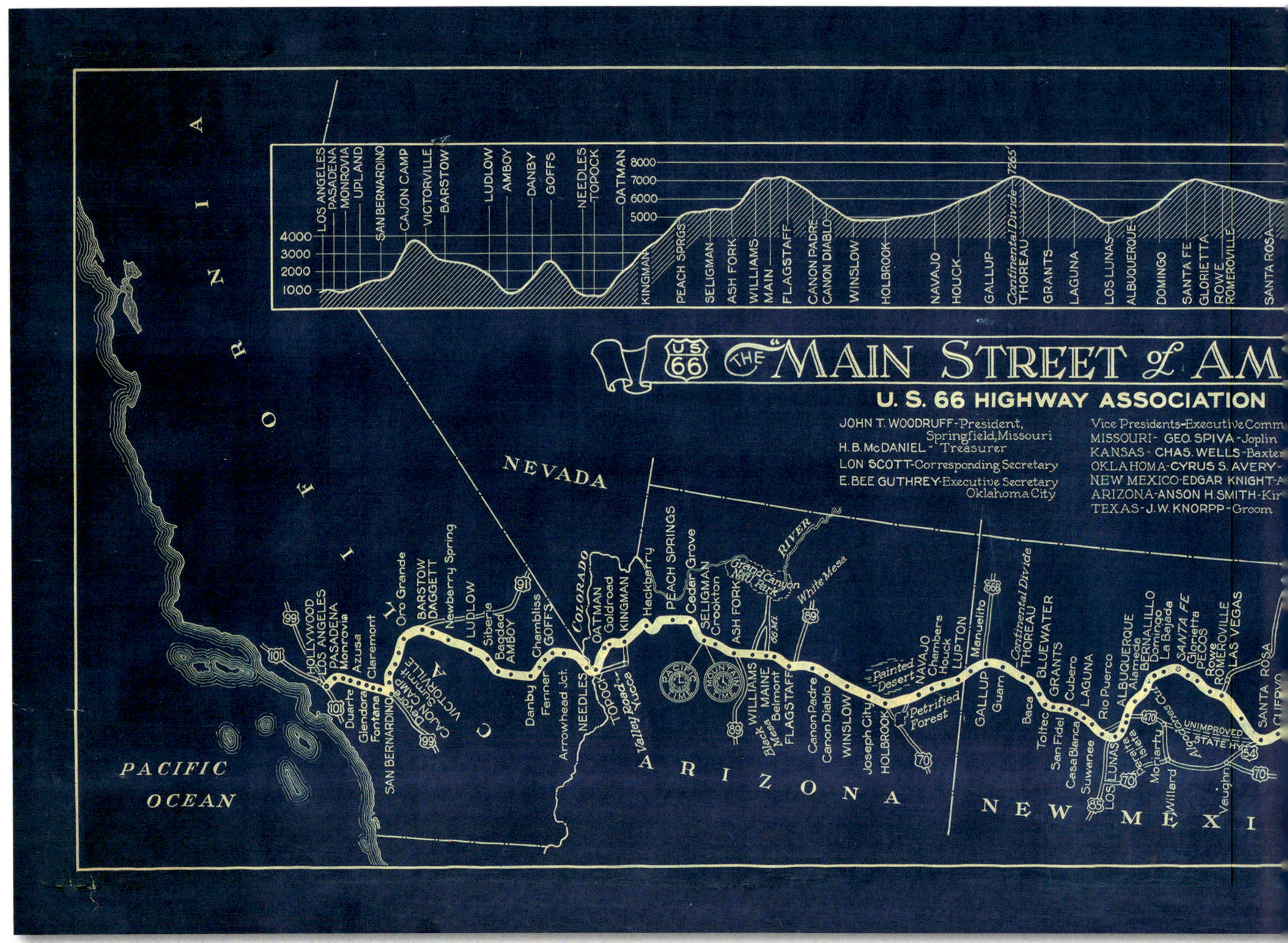

THE "MAIN STREET of AM
U. S. 66 HIGHWAY ASSOCIATION
JOHN T. WOODRUFF-President, Springfield, Missouri
H. B. McDANIEL - Treasurer
LON SCOTT-Corresponding Secretary
E. BEE GUTHREY-Executive Secretary Oklahoma City
Vice Presidents-Executive Comm
MISSOURI - GEO. SPIVA - Joplin
KANSAS - CHAS. WELLS - Baxte
OKLAHOMA - CYRUS S. AVERY -
NEW MEXICO - EDGAR KNIGHT - A
ARIZONA - ANSON H. SMITH - Kir
TEXAS - J. W. KNORPP - Groom
PACIFIC OCEAN
NEVADA
CALIFORNIA
ARIZONA
NEW MEXI

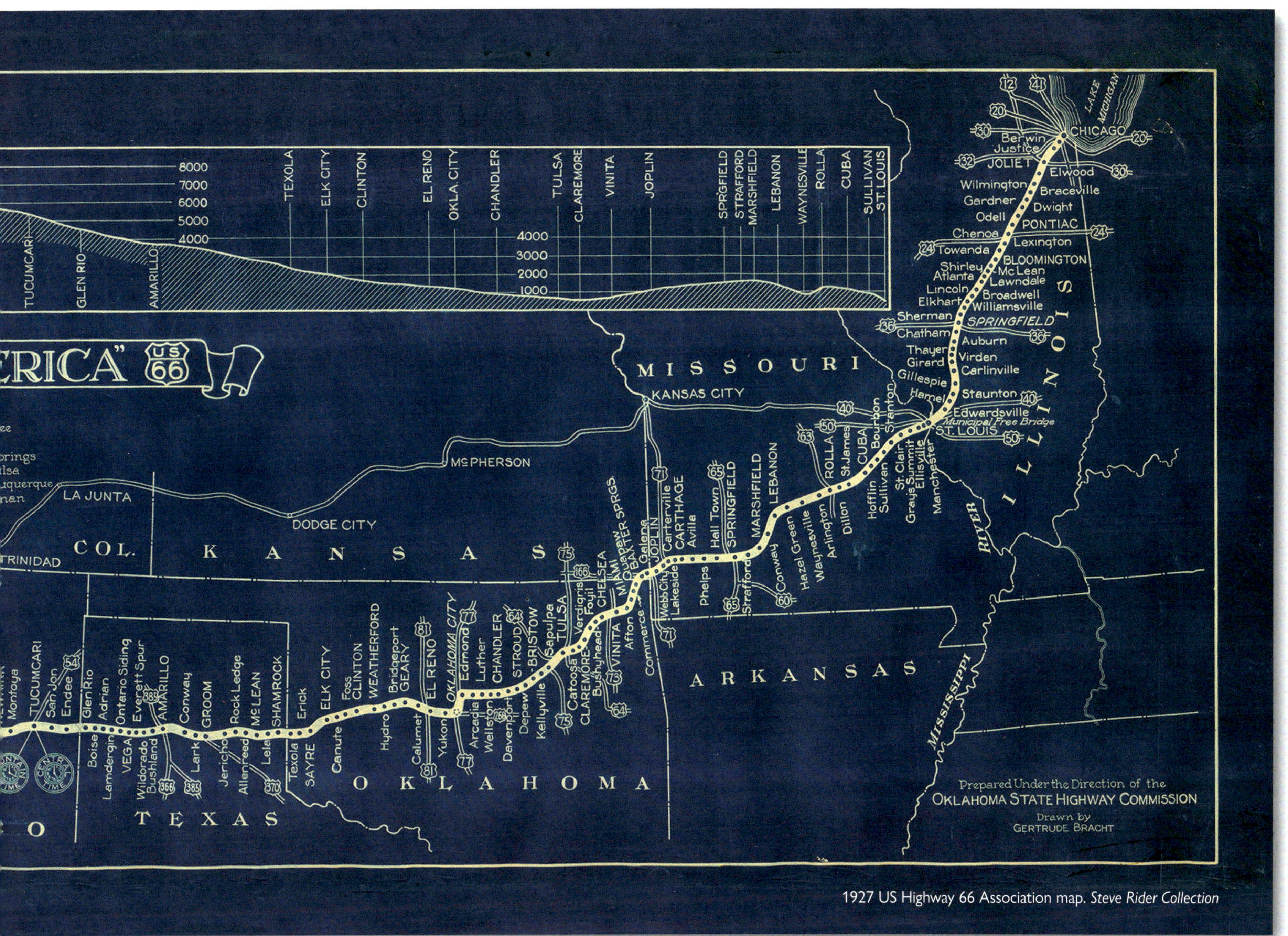

1927 US Highway 66 Association map. *Steve Rider Collection*

Walnut Canyon Creek Bridge, Winona, Arizona.
Norman Wallace Collection, Arizona Historical Society

Contents

Acknowledgments

IRST, A SALUTE to the team at Reedy Press. The confidence they placed in us was inspiring, and the finished product speaks for itself. We couldn't have had a better partner.

The body of work produced by historian Richard Weingroff of the Federal Highway Administration is without equal. Our relationship goes back to the days before personal computers, when he furnished reams of documentation on the history of the US highway system. Needless to say, many of the pages herein contain his fingerprints.

Our wise and trusted friend Michael Wallis expressed his enthusiasm for the book before a word was written and backed it up by offering to write the foreword. His counsel and support over the years are valued treasures that we have relied upon, and benefitted from, time and again.

Road hounds and scholars who must be recognized for their contributions and readiness to lend a hand include Jerry McClanahan, Kathy Anderson, Steve Rider, Mike Ward, Rich Dinkela, Rhys Martin, Trace Hallowell, Kevin and Nancy Mueller, geographer Arthur Krim, and historian T. Lindsay Baker.

The families of players in the Route 66 story went above and beyond in providing photos and information. Among them are Kathy Marmon, widow of Laguna photographer Lee Marmon; descendants of Allen Threatt Sr.; the family of Toonerville's Mary Smeal; Debbie Miller, granddaughter of Bud Rice; Jamie Lawrence, granddaughter of Cynthia and Bobby Troup; Alberta Ellis's grandchildren Irv Logan and Elizabeth Logan Calvin; and Laurrana and Richard Leigon, descendants of Lillian Redman.

The Library of Congress, National Archives, Joe Sonderman's online postcard collection, other public agencies and repositories, and museums were invaluable resources. Archivist Tracie Gieselman France with Missouri State University Libraries located photos and served as liaison with the family of Alberta Ellis. Likewise, filmmaker Katrina Parks furnished background information for others profiled in the Ladies of Legend chapter, and Jillian Hartke, curator of digital collections with the Albuquerque Museum, was intuitive and quick on the draw with requests for historic photographs.

Finally, to the individuals who shared their images from the road, the attributions given with your photos reveal your identities, but not the impact of your collective efforts as photographers and documentarians. Your contributions helped bring the narrative to life, and we are greatly indebted to each of you.

Foreword

HAPPY BIRTHDAY, MOTHER ROAD

ANY PEOPLE consider Route 66 the most famous highway in the United States. I agree. Others claim it may be the best known in the world. I will not argue with them. This much is fact—for me and for tens of thousands of travelers from across the nation as well as visitors from throughout Europe and the Pacific Rim, this fabled American highway will never die.

This path—winding its way through eight states—has evolved into a revered icon. It is a timeless monument to the people who live on its shoulders and for the legions of motorists who travel its length. A trek down the highway is in order for all those who find time sacred and are not in a hurry.

Route 66 is a neon journey down a passageway of memory that helped shape America's history and culture. Driving the highway today not only promises adventure but also evokes feelings of fantasy and romance and gives the traveler a sense of personal involvement. It remains America's Main Street.

Whispers from the road fuel my dreams. I hear the poetry in that pavement—the poetry of 18-wheelers, purring Harleys, sputtering Model Ts, Jeeps, Corvettes, Greyhound buses, the conversations of hitchhikers, and the songs from cowboy camps and hobo fires at suppertime.

Thanks to the waitresses, truckers, grease monkeys, cops, salesmen, GIs, tramps, dreamers, and seekers of magic. Thanks to all who have ever touched this road of broken and fulfilled dreams, this road of myth and legend, this road of our fathers and mothers, the road of our youth.

As the Mother Road turns 100 years old on November 11, 2026, the nation and far beyond celebrates the auspicious occasion.

This book serves as a fitting birthday present for the old road. Each word and image—delivered gift-wrapped from a pair of exceptional storytellers—is a tribute to the past, present, and future of Route 66.

Jim Ross and Shellee Graham are dedicated advocates for the highway. Both have previously researched and published books about Route 66 that have earned awards and accolades and established their place as preservation authorities.

They reside just east of Arcadia, Oklahoma, on a stretch of road that carried original Route 66 traffic from 1926 to 1952 and was placed on the National Register of Historic Places in 1999. Jim designed their home, inspired by a 1930 brick Phillips 66 cottage-style service station.

In 2017, as fellow road warriors gathered to enjoy their collection of neon signs, the crowd was surprised when Jim and Shellee took their vows at a wedding ceremony I was honored to officiate.

I hope you think of Jim and Shellee after you read this book. Perhaps you will encounter them on the road or have a chance to see their neon garden. Remember that they live by the belief that the journey, not the destination, is what really matters. Like me, they want you to experience the America that used to be—America before the nation became generic.

So please click off the cell phone and ease up on the gas pedal. Enjoy the ride.

— Michael Wallis

Pulitzer Prize-nominated author of Route 66: The Mother Road

Max Ortega's Indian Trail Trading Post at Lupton, Arizona, 1950s.
Steve Rider Collection / Color by Shellee Graham

Arizona's Jack Rabbit Trading Post, circa 1950. *Mike Ward Collection*

Preamble

THE LEGEND

Route 66 composer Bobby Troup en route to California, 1946. *Troup Family Archives*

ROM ITS beginning, Route 66 embodied the fusion of automobiles with the lure of the open road, an explosive mix propelled by a pair of sassy sixes. As the gateway to the West, it supercharged the itch to travel, igniting a surge in motoring mania that sent tremors across the land. *Route 66*. The name alone suggests discovery and intrigue. It ferried the desperate and the daring and became a subject for artists, authors, musicians, and filmmakers. It was an escape for both rich and poor, the wise and the foolhardy, dreamers, drifters, poets, and bandits. It produced heroes and villains, both itinerant and home-grown, and it reshaped the human landscape of 20th-century America.

Many followed the route to triumph or tragedy, either scarred from careening off-course or becoming enriched with unforgettable memories to be passed down through generations. Early "autoists" yearning for excitement eagerly hit the road. Close behind were thousands of not-so-eager families fleeing dust-blown farms in haggard jalopies. When Hitler rose from hell, war brides honeymooned on the route, some of them never to see their soldiers again. Survivors of that war embraced a futuristic trend in travel and brought prosperity and vitality to US 66, making it the "vacation highway" for more than two decades. By then, the route was enshrined in the hearts of America.

From the simplicity of a soothing breeze in the shade of a roadside park to the unforgettable candy-colored pulse of neon at a cozy motor court, Route 66 left its mark on millions. During its heyday, the cry of "Are we there yet?" was a refrain parents would forget no sooner than their youngsters would forget the metallic clack of a frosty Grapette pulled from a nickel machine. The twangy slap of a greasy spoon's screen door, lunch from a picnic basket, or driving through a rumbling summer storm would long be remembered.

As the centerpiece of a literary classic and the subject of a jazzy anthem and hit television show, Route 66 symbolized a young nation embracing the auto age with optimism and verve. It became as rooted in American culture as our most revered monuments and now stands as a spiritual passage to the past, its patina a reflection of all who explored its reaches or lived and worked along its worn and wonderous path.

Route 66. Never static, it continues to evolve, flexing and shifting with the winds of change. It led the way in defining America on the move, from the Great Depression and Dust Bowl years through World War II and the ensuing rush to the future. Legend and folklore run deep here. For 100 years it has channeled legions of motorists toward new horizons, becoming the unbreakable thread linking places and people with the times of their lives.

Route 66. One hundred years. And counting.

The Dixie Truckers Home in McLean, Illinois, serving motorists since 1928. *66postcards.com*

Migrants on the move near Bakersfield, California, in 1936. *Dorothea Lange, Library of Congress*

Joe Altobello (left) and two fellow soldiers hitchhiking, 1940s. *Courtesy of Joe Altobello's grandson Bill Clift*

Gas pump handle.
Authors' Collection

Vintage Linco Gasoline sign.
Authors' Collection

Gas was sold at general stores in the early years of automobiles.
Authors' Collection

Corner Front Street and Third Avenue, Yucca, Ariz. On Valley Cut-Off Highway

Members of the Bankhead Highway and Good Roads Associations pose with President Coolidge (center front) at the White House in 1924.
Library of Congress

CHAPTER 1

Revolutionizing Travel

EFORE AUTOMOBILES, venturing more than short distances from one's birthplace was uncommon. Cradle to coffin, experiencing distant lands came mostly through stories told and the printed page. Exceptions were the pioneers in covered wagons and those with the means to book passage on steamships or rail lines. Life, for the most part, was geographically restricted, with mobility generally limited to the range of a horse and buggy.

The first "horseless carriages" in the US were introduced in the late 1800s, but there were no gas stations until around 1905. Before that, travelers hauled gasoline in cans filled at general stores or blacksmith shops. Getting from town to town involved planning, and one had to know where the next source of fuel might be.

Pathways adopted in part by what would become US 66 included ancient Indian trails, the Santa Fe Trail, El Camino Real, the 1858 Beale Wagon Road, the Ozark Trails, and the National Old Trails Road. The earliest routes had been forged by Native Americans, explorers, scouts, and surveyors as passageways between centers of trade and as ways to navigate forbidding terrain. The railroads shadowed these routes, which in turn were followed by auto trails of the early 1900s.

The quest for improved roads began not with automobilists, but with bicyclists, who in 1880 formed the League of American Wheelmen in Newport, Rhode Island. Their efforts led to the Good Roads movement, which rapidly gained momentum and spread across the country. With the dawn of the 20th-century, automobile use was on the rise, and in 1908 Henry Ford's introduction of the Model T lit the fuse on the future of transportation. While initially out of reach for most families at $850, improved mass production slashed that price to $260 by 1924. Predictably, the demand for tolerable driving surfaces—already burning the ears of bureaucrats—grew louder.

Organizations within the Good Roads movement had given rise to a network of named auto trails, many of them extending

Bicycle enthusiasts pose for a portrait in Joliet, Illinois, circa 1885. *Authors' Collection*

Henry Ford's 1908 Model T automobile. *Public domain, photographer unknown*

Red Crown Gasoline sign. *Authors' Collection*

Early camping guide to the Jefferson Highway.
Cameron Historical Society & Depot Museum, Missouri

Historic Lincoln Highway marker at Orr's Ranch, Utah.
Courtesy of Jim Ross

Lady travelers posing next to a National Old Trails Road sign post before highways had numbers.
Jim Farber Collection

beyond state lines. Notable among them were the transcontinental Lincoln and Bankhead Highways and the National Old Trails Road. Building and marking them was funded with membership dues collected from townships and businesses eager to cultivate traffic. Many had provincial or catchy names like the Dixie Highway, Lonestar Route, or Cannon Ball Trail. Their proliferation was such that travelers were ultimately confronted with a chaotic tangle of roadways and intersections clogged with directional arrows. By the 1920s, more than 200 named trails decorated the land. Identifying markers painted on barns, poles, and the like soon weathered, and road maintenance was poor.

Reaching this point was inevitable. Auto ownership mushroomed between 1910 and 1920 from roughly one-half million to ten million. A critical 1924 *Reno Evening Gazette* piece included the following:

Travelers often camped along the roadside in the early days of auto travel. *Authors' Collection*

"In nine cases out of ten these transcontinental associations are common nuisances and nothing else. They are more mischievous than constructive. And in many instances they are organized by clever boomers who are not interested in building roads but in obtaining salaries at the expense of an easily beguiled public."*

The *Tombstone Epitaph* was less polite, describing association leaders as "blood-suckers who have sat in their swivel-chairs and milked the public for funds to keep their swivels greased."

But the sword had two edges. In offering its opinion on a proposed new system of numbered federal highways in 1924, *Western Highways Builder* magazine stated: "Of all the idealistic proposals yet advanced for the administration of highways, none can equal this for pure imbecility."**

In spite of poor road conditions, limited services, and the prospect of breakdowns, motorists showed little reluctance in undertaking long-distance trips, yearning as they were to be "going somewhere." Engines overheated and burned oil, tires went flat, and electrical systems failed. Fuel was gravity-fed, causing stalls on steep hills that could only be remedied using reverse gear. Travelers carried tools, patching kits, innertubes, water, oil, spare fuel, and a token of luck to reach destinations without serious delays. Many of those venturing beyond a day's drive packed kettles and bedding and camped under starry skies at convenient pullouts or roadside camps.

Common was the experience of Iowan James Barclay's aunt and uncle, who mailed him a postcard on September 4, 1923, from Santa Fe, New Mexico, which read: "Arrived here today after three days of driving over the worst roads you ever heard of. In two places bridges entirely gone and all tourists had to be pulled across with teams!"

Drivers relied on the Automobile Blue Book, Automobile Club of Southern California maps, and similar publications to reveal locations of services and help keep them on track. A typical entry from the 1917 Blue Book between Santa Fe and Albuquerque reads: "8.7 Four corners, sign on far right; turn left, passing several adobe houses. Cross RR 9.5, following winding road along edge of hill."

Author and educator Dallas Sharp and his wife, Daphne, motored from Massachusetts to California

Katie Ramori Piazza stands next to a gas pump at the Ramori store in Rosati, Missouri. *Courtesy of Deanna Bokinsky and the Marchi Family*

The 1925 edition of the Mohawk Hobbs Guide. *Authors' Collection*

in December, circa 1925. In 1928, Dallas published a book about their trip, *The Better Country*. They picked up future US 66 near Las Vegas, New Mexico, and followed the mostly unimproved roadway all the way to California. They described the dangerous switchbacks of La Bajada Mesa, and had this to say about driving conditions west of Grants: "In and out of ruts, over the hubs through mire and muck, up on rocks and down into chuck holes, swaying, twisting, pitching, ploughing ahead with churning wheels."

Symbols for named trails.
Authors' Collection

Warning sign for pre-Route 66 motorists at New Mexico's La Bajada Mesa.
Rich Dinkela Collection

The steep, hairpin turns on the early descent at La Bajada Mesa presented a serious hazard.
Steve Rider Collection

The Sharps navigated the harrowing in-and-out of Arizona's Canyon Diablo at night, bore witness to another car sliding over the edge of the fearsome Oatman Road, and had no praise for California's Mojave in San Bernardino County: "Perhaps there is a larger county in the United States and a worse road, though neither proposition is conceivable."

Such tribulations defined life on the road. At the federal level, the Agriculture Department's Bureau of Public Roads (BPR) had been established in 1905 (originally as the Office of Public Roads), but funding for infrastructure lagged. Solutions were needed to make roads more durable and easier to navigate, but the wheels of government turned slowly. In 1914, the American Association of State Highway Officials (AASHO) was formed, and in 1916 the $75 million Federal Aid Road Act was passed by Congress, providing funds for the first time. While limited in scope to improving rural free delivery (RFD) postal routes, it was an important evolutionary step.

The "Roaring Twenties," as they came to be known, were fueled by a curious blend of prosperity and turbulence. Even as the ink dried on the 18th Amendment banning liquor, cultural aberrations spread like illicit whiskey from toppled barrels. Despite Prohibition, society's carefree slogan was "anything goes," giving rise to flappers in raccoon coats, marathon dance contests, Tommy gun-toting gangsters, bootleggers, and G-Men. Speakeasies jammed with tipsy crowds danced the Charleston while swilling outlawed beverages. Corruption rocked Warren Harding's abbreviated presidency, and the Tulsa race massacre brought shame to civility. It was a freewheeling decade of indulgence and upheaval that was stopped only by the stock market implosion in 1929.

Beyond the social bedlam, the nation's highways demanded attention, and the 1920s were pivotal years. The 1916 Road Act was revised in 1921 to include funds for a system of federal aid highways. Initially, those dollars were distributed directly to individual counties, where

A family in their touring car pauses in Oatman, Arizona, in 1916, undeterred by the general state of roads at the time.
Jim Farber Collection

Prior to paving, getting stuck was an expected part of motoring.
Authors' Collection

Brick pavers are used to surface a road near Springfield, Illinois, in the 1920s. *66postcards.com*

they were used to purchase new rights of way, build bridges, and help keep roadways graded and passable. Emerging state highway departments were then granted jurisdiction in doling out those funds and began developing their own highway systems.

Between 1916 and 1922, road projects totaling $189 million were completed, mostly involving graded earth or gravel, though some were hard surfaced. By 1923, federal aid as a source of funding became permanent as auto use continued to expand. Finally, the US government had actively assumed a role in keeping vehicles out of the slop impersonating roads between rains.

Concurrently, plans to devise the first network of numbered highways gained traction. Numbers were already in use on many state highways, demonstrating a more orderly method that previewed the future. The named trails organizations were thus forewarned. Until now they had dominated interstate travel; before the end of the decade, they would face extinction.

The Ozark Trails

WILLIAM HARVEY STARED at the gleaming rails that no longer ferried vacationers to his resort. It was a serious setback, one to be overcome only by converting defeat into opportunity. It was 1910, and service on the five-mile spur he'd built from the St. Louis–San Francisco Line at Lowell, Arkansas, had been discontinued, leaving guests destined for his Monte Ne retreat with no way to get there except by boat. With automobile use on the rise, he envisioned how they might be drawn to the rural northwest corner of the state. Ideas flashed as Harvey eyed the impotent steel, and he suddenly swiveled and strode toward his office, his back turned to the railroad. An audacious solution had materialized, and he needed to put his hands on area maps.

Financier and Ozark Trails Association founder William "Coin" Harvey.
City of Rogers, Arkansas

William Hope "Coin" Harvey was a wealthy lawyer, author, financier, and real estate investor. One of his holdings was a riverside resort he

The clubhouse at Monte Ne's "Missouri Row" hotel. In 2023, the stone tower (left) was the last remaining structure demolished.
Courtesy of Shiloh Museum of Ozark History-David Purdy Collection

The Monte Ne amphitheater consisted of elaborate stone tiers and platforms. It now rests in a watery grave.
Courtesy of Lou Davis Skeen

built near Rogers, Arkansas, at the turn of the 20th century. He named it Monte Ne, for "Mountain Waters," and business was good until the railroad stopped delivering guests. Not one to give up, Harvey spent the next three years turning bad luck into good by capitalizing on the Good Roads movement.

In 1913, Harvey launched the Ozark Trails Association (OTA), a network of roads in Arkansas, Missouri, Kansas, and Oklahoma, with Monte Ne serving as headquarters. Expansion into Colorado, Nebraska, Texas, and New Mexico would follow. Harvey grew the OTA through booster groups and ballyhooed annual conventions

punctuated with motorcades, rousing oratory, politicking, and alcohol-fueled revelry. Attending delegates elected officers, campaigned for new branches, and lobbied to host future meetings. Membership flourished, evidenced by convention attendance in 1916, when over 7,000 OTA delegates rallied in Oklahoma City.

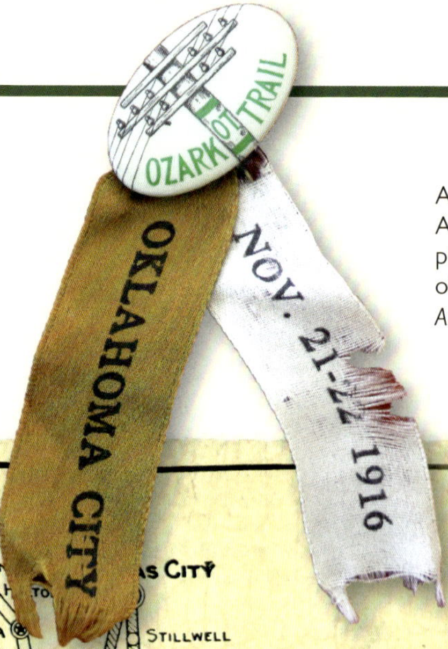

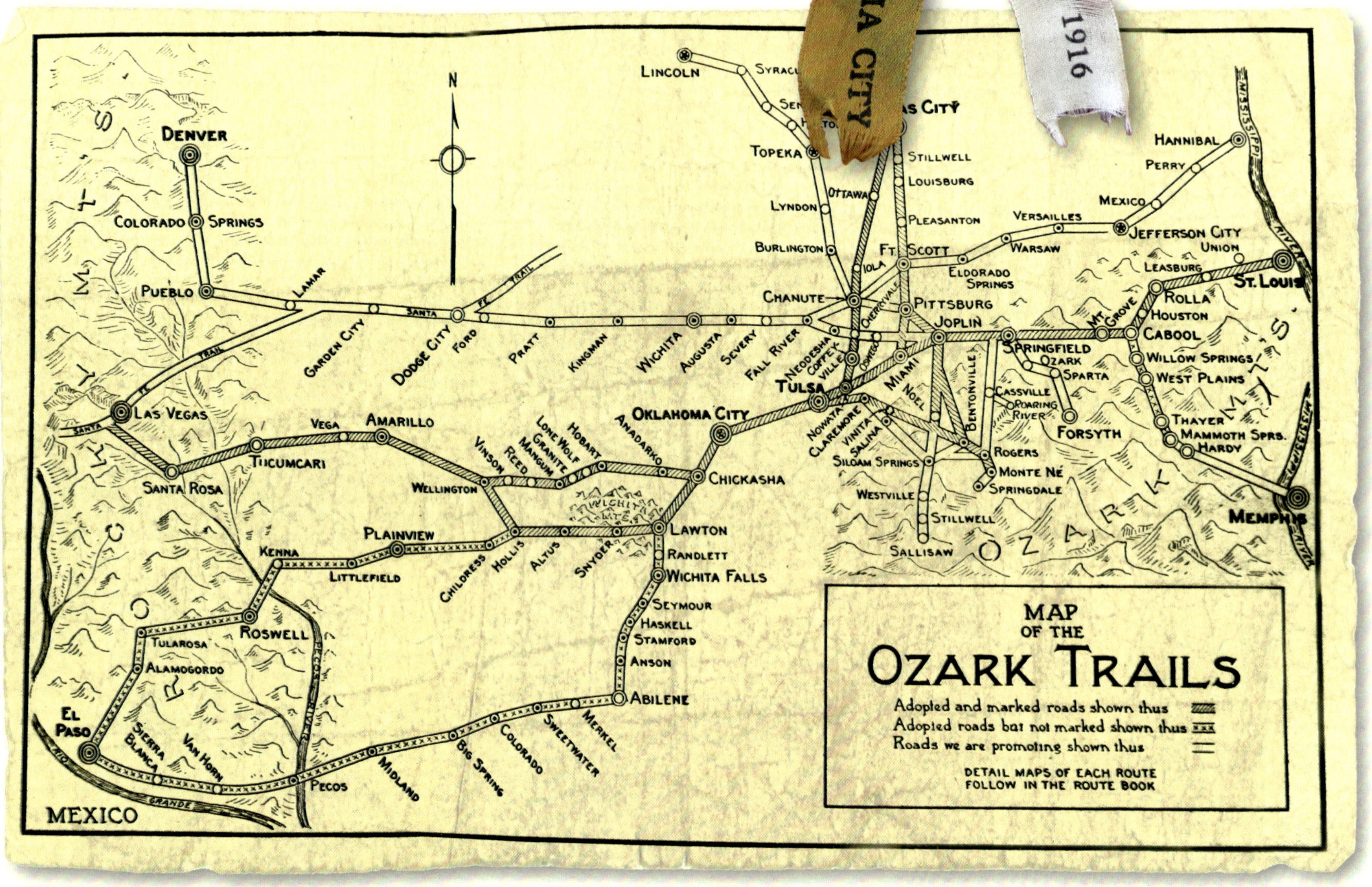

A 1916 Ozark Trails Association Convention pin and overview map of the OT network. *Authors' Collection*

This Ozark Trails obelisk was at the junction with the Santa Fe Trail near Las Vegas, New Mexico.
Authors' Collection

The network's trunk route was finalized the next year at the Amarillo, Texas, convention after contentious debate. It linked St. Louis with Las Vegas, New Mexico, via Springfield, Tulsa, Oklahoma City, Amarillo, and Tucumcari, with spurs to Monte Ne and multiple other branches. To distinguish the Ozark Trails, in 1918 Harvey called for the installation of 20-foot-tall concrete obelisks to serve as navigational aids at important junctions on the network's main line. They carried the green and white Ozark Trails logo and featured directional arrows, town names, and distances. Only 12 of the lofty monuments were planned, but they proved so popular that at least four dozen were built, many on branch routes.

Unfortunately, Harvey was either unwilling or unable to exercise

restraint, and measured control of the network was gradually lost. Dozens of new branches were nominated with little forethought. Some were approved, and some weren't. Some were later marked, and others weren't. By 1920, Harvey's creation had morphed into a disorganized, spidery snarl. Worse, the OTA's matrix of roads was woefully documented. Only two route books were published—in 1918 and 1919, both before multiple changes took place. Harvey eventually stepped down, but the OTA's unraveling was underway even as obelisks were still going up. By 1924, the OTA had quietly disbanded.

Coin Harvey retired to Monte Ne, where he died in 1936. In the 1960s, when the White River was dammed, most of his beloved resort slowly disappeared under the rising waters of Beaver Lake. Surviving structures above the waterline and those exposed at low-water marks were later removed, leaving nary a trace of the OTA's birthplace.

The second and last Ozark Trails Route Book, published in 1919. *Authors' Collection*

These ruins of Monte Ne at Beaver Lake have since been removed. *Courtesy of Matt Miller*

One of seven surviving Ozark Trails obelisks and the only one on Route 66, near Stroud, Oklahoma.
Courtesy of Jim Ross

The preserved Ozark Trails obelisk in Dimmitt, Texas.
Courtesy of Jim Ross

The Good Roads movement was the springboard for modern highways, but after 1926 the named trails organizations were out of business, their colorful signposts replaced with standardized, numbered shields. The OTA, like most of its companions, would have been destined for obscurity except for two things: its relationship with US 66 and its surviving obelisks.

With few deviations, lengthy portions of the Ozark Trails became US 66, including the route from St. Louis, Missouri, to Oklahoma City, and from Amarillo, Texas, to its terminus at the junction with the Santa Fe Trail near Las Vegas, New Mexico. From that point westward, Route 66 assumed the path of the National Old Trails Road.

Most of the OTA obelisks were summarily dismantled and discarded or buried where they stood. Seven of them survive. Only one, near Stroud, Oklahoma, is on the route. The others are at Langston, Oklahoma; in Texas at Wellington, Tampico, Tulia, and Dimmitt; and at Lake Arthur, New Mexico. All of these imposing monuments were built in small communities, and all but two have been restored as historic landmarks. They now represent the legacy of the Ozark Trails and their relationship with US 66. Barring acts of God or man, they will stand in testament to the days of early auto trails for generations to come.

Bureau of Public Roads Chief Thomas H. MacDonald with prototype US Highway shields in 1925. *Library of Congress*

CHAPTER 2

Dueling Numbers

HE FUTURE father of Route 66 was furious. He had worked too hard developing the first system of uniformly numbered highways to be bushwhacked at every turn by one disgruntled individual. Cy Avery's fight with Kentucky governor William Fields had been long and contentious. Now it was mid-March 1926, and Avery had just learned that AASHO president Frank Page had informed Executive Secretary W. C. Markham that everyone on the numbering committee except for Missouri's B. H. Piepmeier was "pleased" with Governor Fields's suggested change. Avery was anything but "pleased," and to suggest otherwise was outrageous. "I propose to fight this to the last ditch," he seethed in a letter to Page.

Cyrus Stevens Avery, the father of Route 66. *A Standard History of Oklahoma, Volume III, 1916*

Tulsa businessman, civic leader, and good roads advocate Cyrus Stevens Avery (1871–1963) had held a leadership position with the OTA and served as president of the Associated Highways of America. In 1923, he was appointed by Governor Martin E. Trapp to chair Oklahoma's new highway commission. Avery assembled a staff of four, including John M. Page for his chief engineer, whom he recruited from the BPR's Fort Worth office. Page's selection was a fateful choice, as he would later play a pivotal role in the saga of numbering US 66.

In 1924, Avery attended an AASHO meeting in San Francisco where a proposal for a national system of numbered routes was formally introduced. The following spring he was appointed by Secretary of Agriculture Howard M. Gore to a 21-member joint board charged with creating the new network of highways under the supervision of BPR design chief E. W. James. Avery also served

Oklahoma Governor Martin E. Trapp.
George Grantham Bain Collection, Library of Congress

Bureau of Public Roads Design Chief E. W. James.
Federal Highway Administration

Oklahoma Highway Commission, 1927.
Oklahoma Department of Transportation Annual Report

B. H. Piepmeier of Missouri.
Missouri Department of Transportation

Frank T. Sheets of Illinois.
Illinois Department of Transportation

Charles H. Moorefield of South Carolina.
South Carolina Department of Transportation

Roy Alton Klein of Oregon.
Courtesy of Doris Klein Moore

on a select committee, chaired by James, charged with mapping the new routes and assigning their numbers. Other select committee members were B. H. Piepmeier of Missouri, Frank Sheets of Illinois, Charles Moorefield of South Carolina, and Roy Klein of Oregon. For the assertive Avery, it was a prime assignment, giving him broad authority in shaping the most prominent highways.

The Joint Board worked throughout the summer of 1925 to link hundreds of existing roads into a network of interstate routes. Within the committee of five, it was Avery who sought to include a major thoroughfare from Chicago to Los Angeles crossing his home state. He was aided in this effort by members Sheets and Piepmeier. The impact of such a highway could not be foretold, but the ulterior motives behind its chosen path would not go unnoticed.

Initially, Avery's proposed route found little acceptance with the full board. It was far removed from known travel corridors such as the Santa Fe Trail or Butterfield Stage route, and it failed to follow either a north–south or east–west orientation, which was the agreed-upon template. It was a hybrid, angling southwesterly from Chicago to Oklahoma City, where it turned west to California, generally along the paths of the Ozark Trails and National Old Trails Road. Resistance to this odd configuration was overcome with the backing of Piepmeier and Sheets, but only after considerable debate.

Once the new highways were mapped, all that remained was the assignment of numbers. It had been agreed that east–west roads would carry even numbers, while north–south roads would carry odd numbers. At the northern US border, east–west routes would begin with US 2 and ascend numerically southward. North–south routes would begin with US 1 on the east coast and ascend numerically westward. The more prominent routes would end in either zero or one. Only short roads or branches would use three-digit numbers, US 101 being an exception.

In September 1925, AASHO's joint board submitted its recommendations to James at the BPR. James approved the plan without delay and in October announced it to the press. Acting on an earlier suggestion by joint board member Lou Boulay of Ohio, highway signs would be modeled after the United States shield.

With their work completed, Avery and company might have quietly slipped into history's black hole of anonymity but for one ironic occurrence—the bitter but doomed fight to keep the assigned number US 60 for the Chicago–Los Angeles route. The committee had chosen the prestigious zero-ending number based on the highway's length and importance. They had no reason to expect opposition, but it came like an assassin's bullet, and from a formidable source.

Kentucky Governor William Fields. *Kentucky Historical Society*

Kentucky governor William J. Fields was not one to slight, and when he learned that those in charge of marking the new federal highways had tossed what he considered table scraps in the direction of his great state, his reaction was explosive. In his thinking, the assignment of the subordinate number 62 to his state's foremost route was an attack on Kentucky's pride, and it was not going to stand.

While Avery was a man of persuasion and orchestrated moves, the governor of Kentucky—in this case at least—showed no inclination toward finesse. It was not lost on him that Avery, Piepmeier, and Sheets had taken the liberty of serving their own states generously. In Avery's case, the new route would conveniently pass directly in front of his own station and cabins in Tulsa. Adding salt to the wound, a Kentucky-based newspaper pointed out that upon reaching Louisville from the east, the state's only road of merit—proposed US 62—scooted off southwesterly through Wickliffe to a terminus in the Missouri hill country where "any tourist who tried to get anywhere on No. 62 would find himself in the middle of the Ozarks with nowhere to go."

The committee took other criticisms and received accolades as well. Facing annihilation, the named trails organizations worked frantically but failed to defeat the new numbering system. Some states protested having too few designations, while one city—St. Louis—crowed at playing host to a bouquet of top-ranked arteries, namely 40, 50, 60, and 61. Despite these apparent inequities, the new highway system was well-received by the public. Except for stamping out sporadic fires of rebellion, as 1925 drew to a close, the Joint Board considered their work to be finished.

Governor Fields, meanwhile, was just getting started. After soliciting support from Kentucky representatives A. B. Rouse and Richard P. Ernst, he decided to simultaneously confront James at the BPR and AASHO Executive Secretary Markham, who formerly had been James's boss at the BPR. A quick look at the map readily revealed that US 20, 30, 40, and 50 ran through states north of Kentucky and that US 70, 80, and 90 ran through states south of Kentucky. US 60, likewise, should have been an east–west road crossing the Bluegrass State. Fields viewed this disorderly bastardization as brazen partisanship, and his demand to James and Markham was straightforward: assign the number 60 to the road from Newport News, Virginia, across Kentucky to a link with the Chicago-Los Angeles road at Springfield, Missouri. This would be a true trans-coastal route consistent with the numbering scheme. It was, he argued, logical and fair. The road from Springfield northward to Chicago could be assigned 62 or another number.

Reaction from Avery and Piepmeier was equally forthright. The finalized map had been approved by the Joint Board and by James. Assigning more than one number to the Chicago–Los Angeles route was unacceptable and non-negotiable. Additionally, they pointed out that their road, though not transcontinental, would carry three times the traffic of that coming from Virginia and deserved the more important number. They could see no reason at such a late hour to redraw the map and flatly refused.

W. C. Markham of the American Association of State Highway Officials. *Federal Highway Administration*

While laying siege to Washington, Fields retaliated in the press. In a December 8, 1925, story published in the *Frankfort* (Kentucky) *Journal*, the governor declared that, "Chicago influence is written all over the [US] Highway map. I particularly object to the obliteration of my idol, my dream, the Midland Trail, running from Ashland to Lexington and to Louisville. I will use every means in my power to fight this proposition of isolation."

The Midland Trail Association was more pointed. In a Louisville-based article titled "U.S. ROAD MAP EFFACES STATE," they claimed that Kentucky had been ". . . virtually erased from the United States road map. As a pacifier, a secondary U.S. numbered road starting at Ashland and ending in the swamps of Arkansas, is offered Louisville. Comparing this meager offering of U.S.-marked roads with our more fortunate sister cities is to blush with shame and humiliation. The policy of silence, concealment and secretiveness of this joint board is un-American and should be universally condemned."

Avery attended an AASHO Executive Committee meeting in Chicago in January 1926, where this and other complaints were discussed. It was finally agreed that Avery's route would retain the number 60 and that 62 would mark the Newport News-to-Springfield highway. This would put Kentucky on a coast-to-coast route, even if it consisted of two separate numbers. During this meeting, Avery remarked that he was less concerned with the number being 60 than with keeping only a single number from Chicago to Los Angeles. Some understood this to mean he would accept 62 if push came to shove. While this was unintended, Avery's words would come back on him like a menacing boomerang.

About the same time, James's boss at the BPR, Thomas H. MacDonald, was swayed by arguments from Governor Fields and congressmen Rouse and Ernst that Avery should settle for US 62, but his change of mind was shortsighted. It gave higher ranking (No. 60) to a road crossing only two-and-a-half states (Newport News, Virginia, to Springfield, Missouri) while downgrading a major route through eight states to a lesser status (No. 62). As expected, word of MacDonald's position hit the select committee like a safe pitched from a rooftop. On February 4, 1926, Piepmeier sent a telegram to Markham:

> WE BITTERLY PROTEST THE CHANGE IN ROUTE NUMBERS SIXTY AND SIXTY TWO STOP CHICAGO TO LOS ANGELES IS THE IMPORTANT ROUTE AND SHOULD CARRY THE ZERO NUMBER STOP WE HAVE PUBLISHED AND DISTRIBUTED SIX HUNDRED THOUSAND MAPS SHOWING NUMBERS AS ORIGINALLY ASSIGNED STOP IT IS IMPOSSIBLE FOR US TO CHANGE THESE NUMBERS.

Four days later Avery wired Markham as well:

IF ROUTES ARE TO BE CHANGED THIS WAY WITHOUT NOTICE TO STATES OR TO EXECUTIVE COMMITTEE YOU ARE MAKING A JOKE OF THE INTERSTATE HIGHWAY STOP WE SHALL INSIST ON ROUTE SIXTY FROM CHICAGO TO LOS ANGELES.

Markham replied to Avery with some annoyance, pointing out that Kentucky's delegation struck the deal with MacDonald at the BPR, not AASHO. He then assured Avery that no final action would be taken without Executive Committee approval. MacDonald, tiring of the distraction, wrote to Avery on March 30. "I do not feel that it makes one bit of difference to the states . . . whether it is Route No. 60 or 62 or any other number so long as the number is carried continuously, and that has been conceded," clearly alluding to Avery's concessionary comments at the January meeting in Chicago.

Other storms were brewing. 1926 was an election year in Oklahoma, and incumbent governor Martin Trapp was trailing challenger Henry Johnston. Should Trapp be defeated, it would mean the end of Avery's appointment. With the calendar looming large, Avery contacted Missouri's Piepmeier to arrange a meeting in Springfield on April 30 for the express purpose of finding a solution to the war over numbers.

Present for the meeting were Avery, Piepmeier, and Avery's engineer, John M. Page. It was held in Superintendent H. B. Mobberly's Division 8 office of the Missouri Highway Department, located in the Greene County Courthouse. As the meeting progressed, it was Page, in reviewing number assignments, who discovered that 66 was not in use, and he suggested it as a possible replacement. Initially it was discussed only briefly, as Piepmeier's position was to hold out for US 60. Avery, however, knew that such a stance would not resolve the standoff, and he felt that the number 66 had a certain appeal. As the afternoon wore on, with no better alternatives found, Piepmeier was persuaded that it was a workable option.

At 4 p.m. that afternoon a telegram was sent from the Colonial Hotel's telegraph office to MacDonald at the BPR informing him of their preference for 66 over 62. Though not their hoped-for outcome, this would allow them to relinquish the number 60 while avoiding the rejected number 62. It would also ensure the use of just one number for the entire route.

With the dispatch of the telegram, Springfield, Missouri, became the symbolic birthplace of the route, even though nothing was settled on that day or for nearly three months thereafter. MacDonald was out of the country, and Markham could not act, either, as he was attending to his wife's illness. Upon MacDonald's return in May, Avery spelled it out for him in a letter. "We are willing at this time to accept 66 or US 60 with the strict understanding that the road from Springfield, Missouri, through Kentucky to Newport News does not carry the same number either as North or South, East or West, A or B road. We are willing to proceed to put up our US Markers, either US 60 or 66."

The answer came to Avery in Tulsa on July 23, and it came from AASHO's Markham rather than MacDonald at the BPR. "If you will assign number 60 to the route from the Atlantic Coast to Springfield, Missouri, Kentucky will then be satisfied with the assignment of the number 66 to the route from Chicago via Springfield to Los Angeles." Approval would become official through an AASHO Executive Committee vote on August 6.

Missouri and Oklahoma had to junk signs and maps for US 60 already manufactured, but Avery succeeded in clearing the last hurdle before being forced from office. On November 11, at the national AASHO meeting in Pinehurst, North Carolina, the

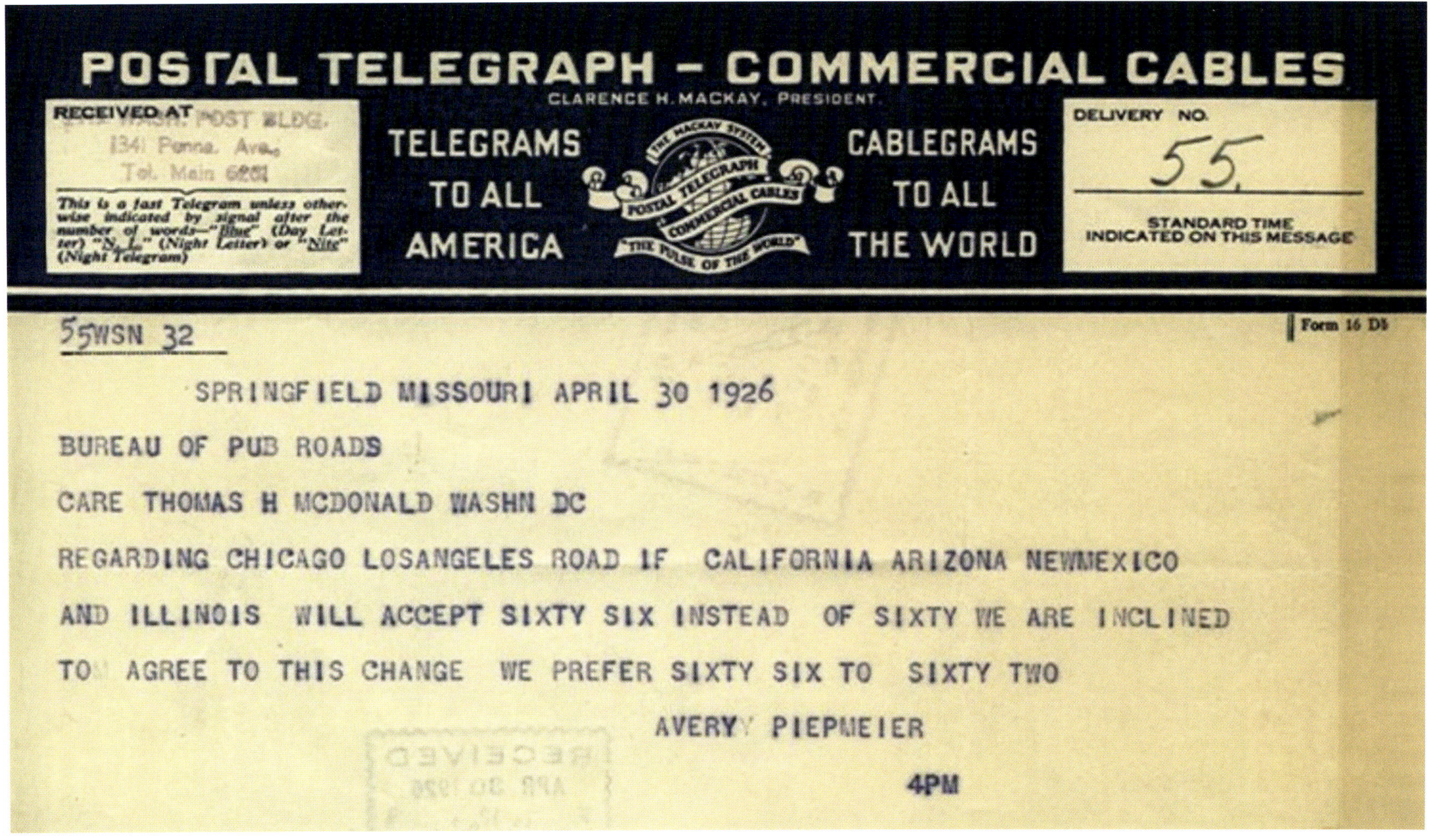
POSTAL TELEGRAPH - COMMERCIAL CABLES
CLARENCE H. MACKAY, PRESIDENT.
RECEIVED AT POST BLDG.
1341 Penna. Ave.
Tel. Main 6281
This is a fast Telegram unless otherwise indicated by signal after the number of words—"Blue" (Day Letter) "N.L." (Night Letter) or "Nite" (Night Telegram)
TELEGRAMS TO ALL AMERICA
CABLEGRAMS TO ALL THE WORLD
DELIVERY NO. 55.
STANDARD TIME INDICATED ON THIS MESSAGE
55WSN 32
Form 16 DS

SPRINGFIELD MISSOURI APRIL 30 1926

BUREAU OF PUB ROADS

CARE THOMAS H MCDONALD WASHN DC

REGARDING CHICAGO LOSANGELES ROAD IF CALIFORNIA ARIZONA NEWMEXICO AND ILLINOIS WILL ACCEPT SIXTY SIX INSTEAD OF SIXTY WE ARE INCLINED TO AGREE TO THIS CHANGE WE PREFER SIXTY SIX TO SIXTY TWO

AVERY PIEPMEIER

4PM

The Springfield Telegram, which led to the end of the numbering controversy.
National Archives

uniform numbering system was formally adopted by all the states and the first official map featuring the new network of federal aid highways was released.

Fields won the prized number 60, though initially its reach westward was only as far as Springfield, Missouri. (Later, US 60 would be extended from Springfield all the way to a junction with I-10 near Quartzsite, Arizona, while the unwanted US 62 ended up stretching from Niagara Falls, New York, to El Paso, Texas.)

Avery and Piepmeier lost what they had fought strenuously to keep, but were winners in a way far greater than either could have imagined. For on the 11th day of November 1926, their Chicago-to-Los Angeles thoroughfare—that misfit, rebel road forever branded with a pair of rhythmic sixes—took up residence on the American landscape.

The Bunion Derby

ANDY PAYNE COUGHED against the swirling clouds of dust puffed up by passing cars. It stuck to his sweat-slicked skin like whitewash on weathered wood. His tank-top shirt with the number 43 stitched to the front was soaked and stained, and the ache in his feet was brutal, but even that paled against the heat searing his shoulders and neck. The sun was at high arc, promising no relief for hours to come. He knew going in that it would come down to stamina and willpower. The pack of runners had thinned considerably, but with so many competing it would have to thin a good deal more. Later he would nurse his swollen feet, elevate them for the night, then do it all again tomorrow and for days on end. For now, he set his mind adrift and focused on planting one foot in front of the other.

Flamboyant sports promoter C. C. "Cash & Carry" Pyle.
Public Domain via Wikimedia Commons

Andy Payne at the Ascot Speedway in Los Angeles prior to starting the race.
From a Solomon Sir Jones Film made for C. C. Pyle. Public domain

* * *

Route 66 Association publicist Lon Scott knew that making US 66 America's premier highway would take more than brochures and advertising. It needed an event, one that would draw the eyes of the nation, and what he had in mind was to stage a 3,400-mile footrace from Los Angeles to New York that would include all of US 66. It was a bold gamble, but with association backing and the recruitment of nationally known sports promoter C. C. "Cash & Carry" Pyle, it was soon scheduled for the spring of 1928. Pyle enthusiastically took charge and quickly lured runners from around the globe, some of them long-distance champions. The dangling carrot was a whopping $25,000 first-place prize.

The race was dubbed "C. C. Pyle's 1st Annual International Transcontinental Footrace," but would become known as the "Bunion Derby" due to the beating taken by the runners' feet. Athletic shoes of the era were primitive, and most road surfaces were either unpaved, graveled, or under construction. Entrants ranged in age from 16 to 64, and each ponied

Official Bunion Derby program.
Courtesy of the late Vivian Payne

up a $100 entry fee to be held in escrow for their transportation home.

One unlikely hopeful was Andrew Hartley Payne, a part-Cherokee farm boy from the Route 66 community of Foyil, Oklahoma. A fleet-footed runner in high school, the 19-year-old showed promise, but could claim no competitive wins beyond state track meets. Even so, he was motivated by an opportunity to help pay off the family farm, and he instinctively felt he could win. He diligently trained on the back roads near his home and was helped with donations for the entry fee. His father offered support as well, borrowing money to make sure Andy got his chance.

On March 4, 1928, the assembled crowd at Los Angeles's Ascot Speedway came to its feet as more than 200 runners assumed their starting positions. Applause turned to cheers as football celebrity Red Grange ignited a small bomb to send the entrants circling the track and onto the street. The finish line was New York City's Madison Square Garden, where only the top 10 competitors would receive cash prizes. Accumulated elapsed time between daily start and end points would determine the positions of the runners. Among the many seasoned marathoners whom Payne would have to beat was record holder Arthur Newton of England, the odds-on favorite to win.

Philip Willer of Canada keeps pace with Seattle's Ed Gardner, whose nickname "Sheik" is stenciled across his shirt. *El Reno Carnegie Library*

Twelve contestants dropped out during the first two days, a trend that would continue throughout the ordeal. Crossing the Mojave Desert, runners were relentlessly scorched by an angry sun and scoured by wind-whipped sand. They were afflicted with dehydration and cramps and bedded down at night with tortured feet. Only 155 Bunioneers trudged out of Bagdad, California, a mere 200 miles from Los Angeles.

Newton maintained the lead into Arizona, but it was the unheralded Payne, though still five hours back, who had methodically moved up. Entering Peach Springs, he passed second-place runner Ed "the Sheik" Gardner of Seattle, a powerful but undisciplined athlete who periodically charged to the front only to ease up, as if he could regain lost ground at will. Payne now had only the Englishman to overtake, but how he might have closed that gap will never be known, as the unthinkable happened on the run from Two Guns to Winslow when Newton faltered and had to quit, his legs gone.

Payne inherited the lead, but the next day was stricken with tonsillitis. Seriously weakened, he struggled to stay in the race, watching helplessly as opponents passed him by. It wasn't until the runners were out of Arizona and well into New Mexico that a fully recovered Andy regained lost ground. At Grants, he edged back into second place. But now snapping at his heels was Peter "Iron Man" Gavuzzi, an Italian from Britain who had outpaced the pack

Andy Payne passes spectators with a caravan of supporters trailing behind.
El Reno Carnegie Library

A billboard near St. Louis advertises the race.
Courtesy of the late Vivian Payne

almost unnoticed during a persistent advance.

In another surprise, current leader Arne Souminen of Finland, who had been consistently in the hunt since leaving Los Angeles, crimped an Achilles tendon near Groom, Texas, and was finished. Andy Payne once again owned the lead, drawing the attention of sports reporters coast to coast. Ed Gardner remained a serious rival, but Andy's biggest threat now was Gavuzzi, whose steady gains finally put him out front. Entering his home state, Andy was forced to dial it up as the two leap-frogged each other through Oklahoma and Missouri.

Pyle's tenacious runners were now front-page news. Spectators lined city streets to cheer them on. Stores closed and schools turned out students to witness the spectacle. For those pounding the pavement, the grueling days became a blur, and their numbers continued to dwindle, some from exhaustion, some from injuries. Nearing St. Louis, the roster had thinned to 73 contenders.

The punishing race wore on through Illinois, leaving Route 66 at Chicago to turn eastward. Crossing Indiana, Gavuzzi steadily pulled away, and the outcome of the race appeared decided. Though bewildered, Andy wisely chose to maintain a set pace. He had to stay healthy to finish, even if that meant second place. Then, at the town of Butler, four miles from the Ohio state line, pain blossomed in Gavuzzi's jaw and progressively worsened. It was diagnosed as an

Peter Gavuzzi, who was in a position to win but forced to drop out due to illness. *Ultrarunninghistory.com*

abscessed tooth, and as the infection spread, he became feverish. Two days later, during the run to Fremont, Ohio, Peter Gavuzzi had no choice but to quit the race.

New Jersey's gritty John Salo, another of the frontrunners, now held second place, but he was 20 hours behind Payne, who had only to avoid injury and illness to win. Gardner, meanwhile, had gradually fallen back, either from exhaustion or feeling content to finish in the money.

On May 26, 84 days out of Los Angeles, Andy Payne trotted into Madison Square Garden and into sports history. He was 15 hours ahead of Salo and one of 55 runners to complete the race. Salo earned $10,000. Phillip Granville, a pure walker from Canada, placed third to win $5,000. Fourth place was taken by intrepid Irishman Mike Joyce for $2,500. Fifth, sixth, and seventh places went to Italian Guisto Umek, also a pure walker; Minnesota's William Kerr; and New York's Louis Perrella, each for $1,000. The flamboyant Gardner finished eighth, also for $1,000, followed by Frank VonHue of California and Canadian John Kronick for the same amount. At the start of the race, only Umek and Granville were among odds-makers' favorites to place. Not mentioned were Payne, Gavuzzi, Gardner, or the other top-10 finishers.

New Jersey's John Salo with wife Amelia. Salo took second place. *Ultrarunninghistory.com*

Studio portrait of Andy Payne following the race. *Courtesy of the late Vivian Payne*

C. C. Pyle barely made expenses and was slow to pay his winners. He staged a second race along a different route in 1929, but it failed to generate much interest, and Pyle soon faded from public view. Andy paid off the farm, married his sweetheart Vivian, and after soldiering in World War II served as Clerk of the Oklahoma Supreme Court for 38 years, earning a law degree along the way. The Cherokee Nation, as well as his hometown of Foyil, have recognized him with statues, and annual marathons continue to be held in his honor. Andy Payne never raced again.

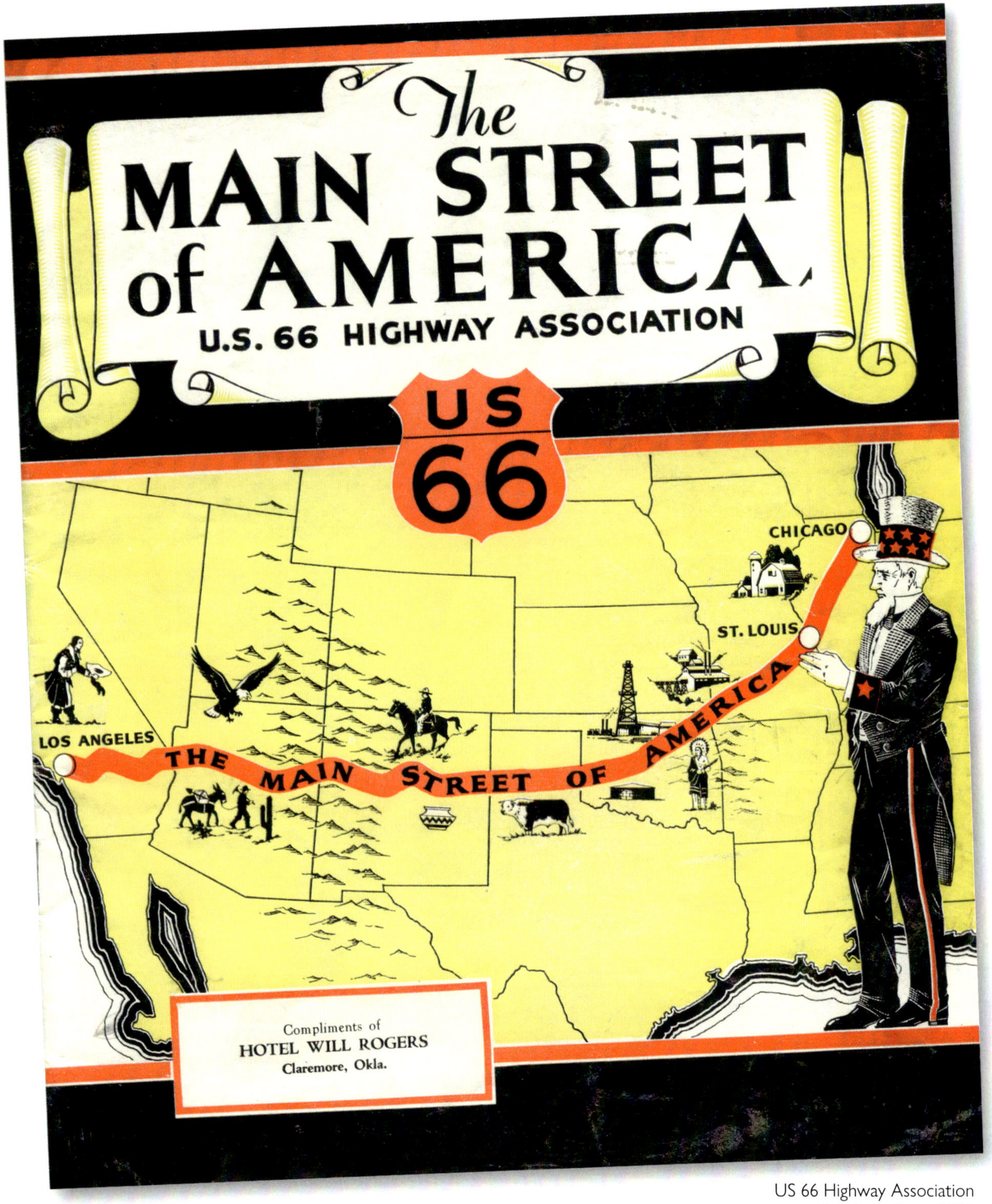

The
MAIN STREET
of AMERICA
U.S. 66 HIGHWAY ASSOCIATION
US
66
CHICAGO
ST. LOUIS
LOS ANGELES
THE MAIN STREET OF AMERICA
Compliments of
HOTEL WILL ROGERS
Claremore, Okla.

US 66 Highway Association Brochure from 1927.
Kathy Anderson Collection

The Willow Street Shell Station in Baxter Springs, Kansas, offered fuel, dry goods, and hot food.
Courtesy of Baxter Springs Historical Society & Heritage Center

During the early years of the route, Klinefelter Camp was one of only a few stops along a hundred miles of desert between Needles and Ludlow, California.
66postcards.com

Rimmy Jim's place near Meteor Crater, Arizona, stocked dry goods and liquor and featured a jukebox and one-armed bandits to help break the desert boredom. Owner "Rimmy" Jim Giddings stands in the right foreground.
Authors' Collection

CHAPTER 3

When Route 66 Was New

T BEGAN as a collection of stitched-together state, county, and local roads. Stretching roughly 2,400 miles, US 66 meandered through eight states, most of it dirt, and it clung to the lay of the land, taking the path of least resistance in the shadow of existing railroads and along section lines separating farms. Motorists encountered mud slicks, chuckholes, steep hills, sudden dips, 90-degree turns, sharp curves, washouts, and spongy shoulders. Signage was still in the works, and rules of the road were mostly determined by drivers. Other than hotels and a scattering of primitive motor courts, options for lodging were roadside camping or one-room cabin rentals. On the upside, access to food and fuel generally wasn't a worry, even in the barren reaches, as most filling stations stocked canned goods, sundries, and liquor, and many had mechanics.

Adoption of the uniform numbering system in November 1926 created an immediate need for maps and highway markers, and getting the route paved end to end was a top priority. As predicted, Cyrus Avery was relieved of his highway commission duties by incoming governor Henry Johnston, but Avery remained an active force, organizing the US Highway 66 Association, which was launched in Tulsa on February 4, 1927.

Elected as the association's first president was John T. Woodruff of Springfield, Missouri. Woodruff was a lawyer, businessman, and civic leader with an impressive track record of promoting better roads. At Avery's suggestion,

Association president John T. Woodruff of Springfield, Missouri. From *Missouri, the Center State*

Brochure from the Arizona Unit of the US Highway 66 Association. *Authors' Collection*

US 66 Booster Club, El Reno, Oklahoma. *Oklahoma Department of Transportation*

the association chose the name Main Street of America for publicity purposes. They published brochures and postcards, organized booster clubs, and fostered relationships with state highway departments. They bought ads in national publications and promoted major attractions and events along the route. One handout from Arizona's Mohave County Chamber of Commerce colorfully described the allure of US 66 as: "The Chosen Thoroughfare of the Discriminating American Tourist . . . Undreamt of . . . Incredible . . . Incomprehensible is the Scenic Grandeur & Beauty of the Trip Over U.S. Highway No. 66."

Motorists responded by taking to the road, disregarding the route's often-dismal conditions. Several stretches, especially in the West, were known to be downright treacherous. One of those was the infamous Jericho Gap in the Texas panhandle, bounded by McLean in the east and Groom to the west. Located about 10 miles east of Groom, the settlement of Jericho began in the late 1800s and became a railroad stop in 1902. By the late 1920s it featured filling stations, cafés, a hotel, and a school. The unpaved roadway there shadowed the railroad, rising and falling with the terrain. The problem was rain, specifically how it converted the soil there into a thick, tire-sucking muck that stopped motorists cold. Its grip was such that oftentimes the only way to break free was to glad-hand a nearby farmer in possession of a tractor and chain.

The designation of a primary US highway should have stimulated growth, but road conditions along the Jericho Gap were so bad that US 66 was moved north by almost a mile when paving arrived in the 1930s, leaving the discarded township as stranded as the hapless motorists often caught in the quagmire there. Even with a connector road to the paved route, decay set in, and Jericho slowly perished.

The ghosts of Jericho now have new guardians, descendants of the Schaffer clan who have preserved its history and what remains of the townsite. In the nearby cemetery are the graves of homesteaders dating to 1895, many of them children. A headstone inscription there for an eight-year-old boy dated 1905 reads: "Twas Hard to Give Thee Up." The same could be said

The Hotel Lyons in Jericho, Texas. *Courtesy of Leann Mitchell*

Repairing the Jericho Gap roadway was an ongoing task in the 1920s. *Courtesy of John Morrow*

The name Schaffer is found throughout Jericho's cemetery. The townsite is now owned and preserved by descendants Blair and Blanca Schaffer. *Courtesy of Blair and Blanca Schaffer*

Donald Crosno poses with La Bajada Hill warning sign at the "improved" point of descent in 1925. *Palace of the Governors Photo Archives*

about the settlement of Jericho, unfairly destined to be scrubbed from the land by the punishing West Texas wind.

Continuing west, travelers experienced a gradual rise in elevation as they neared the Caprock, a steeply sloped drop-off about 15 miles east of the New Mexico state line. This geologic formation serves as a transition point between the high plains of the Llano Estacado (staked plains) and the Mesalands to the west. The panoramic view is enchanting, and the descent once demanded respect, but it was not nearly as troublesome as the obstacle drivers faced at La Bajada Mesa west of Santa Fe.

La Bajada (the descent) impeded travel for over 300 years. By the time the Spanish settlement of La Bajada village was established at its base in the early 1700s, the primitive El Camino Real de Tierra Adentro had been crudely carved into the mesa's escarpment. In the mid-1800s, the US Army made improvements to allow passage of heavy wagons, and stone retaining walls built with convict and Cochiti Indian labor added a further measure of safety. In the early 1900s, it became part of the National Old Trails Road but was still perilous, and the hairpin turns just below the mesa's top proved too severe for long trucks and buses. To solve the problem, the point of descent

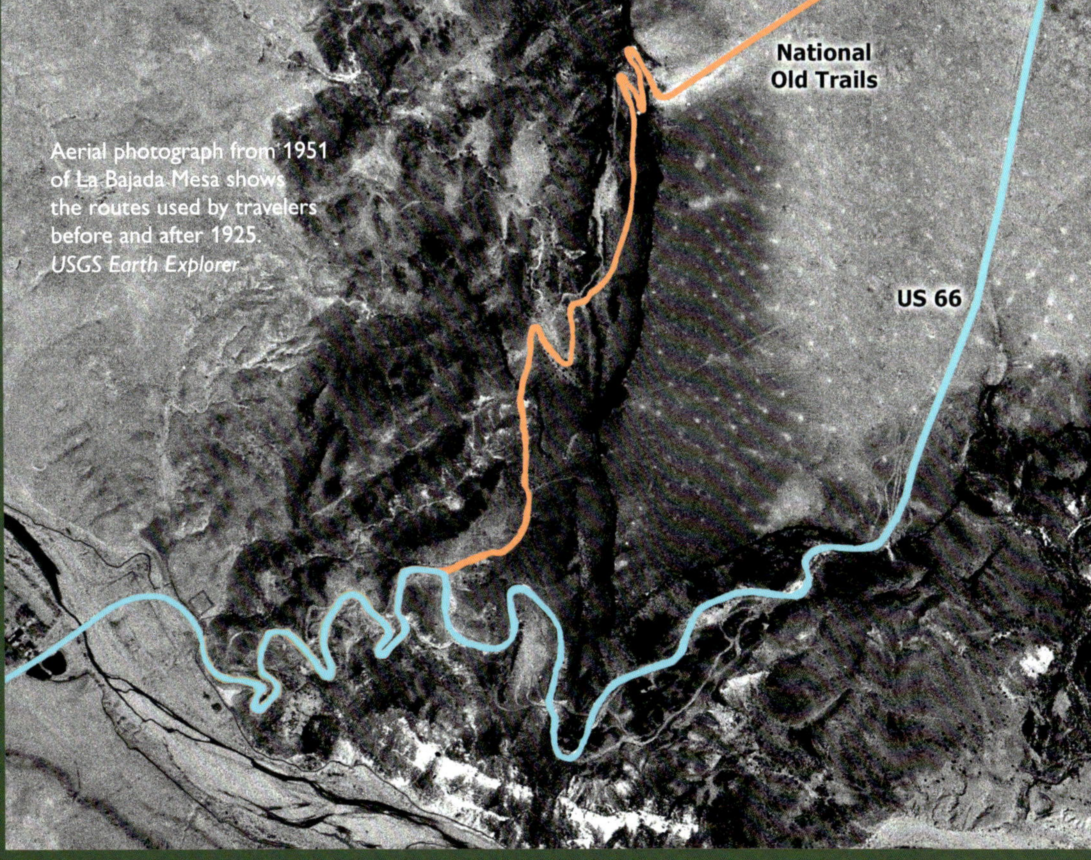

Aerial photograph from 1951 of La Bajada Mesa shows the routes used by travelers before and after 1925. *USGS Earth Explorer*

The Big Cut, built in 1909, was on the El Camino Real between Santa Fe and Albuquerque. *Authors' Collection*

was moved in 1924 to the opposite side of the plateau, where it snaked its way down to join the existing road near the halfway point. In 1926, the revised alignment became US 66.

Even then, navigating La Bajada Mesa was daunting. Westbound travelers confronted a one-mile-long descent with a 600-foot drop in elevation. Heavy rains dug ruts and left a slippery surface; in places, even the use of chains couldn't prevent fishtailing. At the bottom, a timber bridge spanned the Santa Fe River, the point from which eastbound motorists attempted the steep, twisting incline. For those commanding vehicles with gravity-fed fuel pumps, reaching the top could require attacking it in reverse gear, upping the odds of veering off the roadway.

Action was finally taken in 1932 when the highway was moved two miles south to more gently sloped terrain. There it shared its path with US 85 and upwards of a thousand motorists per day who were no longer bullied by switchbacks and a sheer cliff. Only five years later, in 1937, US 66 along the entire Santa Fe loop was replaced by a direct route from Santa Rosa to Moriarty, cutting travel time between the two considerably. The route's former alignment from Santa Fe to Albuquerque, still signed as US 85, later became I-25.

Oatman Road in the Black Mountains of Arizona. *Courtesy of Jim Ross*

Early travelers continued from La Bajada through Albuquerque to Los Lunas, and from there westward toward Arizona. Other than the rigors of negotiating canyons and washouts, it wasn't until roughly 15 miles west of Kingman, Arizona, that another white-knuckle challenge loomed. Here began the ascent through the Black Mountains, a gold-mining region bordering the Colorado River valley. While its grades were slightly better than La Bajada, the switchbacks were tight and in greater numbers, and the circuitous route meandered for 14 miles, eight of those ascending to Sitgreaves Pass before descending the twisty downhill stretch into Oatman. Motorists were gifted with the splendor of scenic rock formations and eye-pleasing vistas, but a trip through the Black Mountains also meant coping with boiling radiators and unforgiving drop-offs that allowed no room for mistakes.

Even crossing the flatlands westward from Oatman required vigilance. Motorists were now in the Mojave Desert, and from

US 66 between Oatman, Arizona, and the Colorado River. View is eastbound toward Oatman. *Courtesy of Jim Ross*

there to the California line, the route was a continual series of dips and rises and unannounced curves. Easily flooded arroyo crossings added to the danger. Safely reaching the Colorado River at Topock brought relief, but getting there offered only a preview of what lay ahead. The Mojave, a vast and barren cooktop, stretches from near Kingman, Arizona, westward for 200 miles. Route 66 avoided none of it, and those who failed to prepare or whose vehicles were last repaired with baling wire or fabricated parts were apt to meet with dire consequences.

Water bags were a necessity when crossing the desert. *Courtesy of Shellee Graham*

The oasis of Needles was reached only 12 short miles into California. West of there, across the Mojave skillet, services were sparse for the next 100 miles, even after paving was completed in the 1930s. Filling stations, some with cabins, were scattered about, but not much else, and drivers had to plan on handling repairs at the point of breakdown. Given the unreliable state of automotive cooling systems, it was imperative to carry water bags and wise to wait until the sun set and temperatures cooled before making the trek. Such was the risk that, during periods of extreme heat, it was advised that pregnant women and children avoid crossing the Mojave during daylight hours.

Early travelers arriving at the Wayside Camp in Essex, California, had access to multiple services. *Authors' Collection*

A road grader spreads asphalt as part of a 1930s paving project. *Oklahoma Department of Transportation*

* * *

The BPR did not attempt to delineate precise pathways for the new numbered highways, leaving individual states to determine turn-by-turn routes. This was only practical, as highway departments were already acquiring new rights of way and streamlining existing roads through previously granted funds. For US 66, uniform paving would occur piecemeal over an 11-year span as dollars became available. During this time, hundreds of changes to the original alignment took place. Efforts were made to reduce the number of railroad grade crossings, correct abrupt curves, and improve flood-prone areas. Standards were updated for roadways and for signage and other traffic control devices. Steel and concrete bridges were built to last a minimum of 75 years.

As might be expected, getting the route paved involved dealmaking at every level by politicians and prominent individuals. Striking a balance between serving the needs of motorists and satisfying those wielding influence made for a rough ride. Travel-guide publishers struggled to keep up.

Disagreements centered most often on bypassing town business districts. Such disputes during this long birthing process most often fell to the BPR and AASHO. An especially bitter fight took place in 1932 between the BPR and Oklahoma State Highway Commission over the bypassing of Wellston, Oklahoma. The state had assured city leaders that the permanent alignment of US 66 would pass through downtown. Now, with paving at its doorstep, the BPR dictated that it continue due west from the approach to the town, circumventing the business district by almost a mile. The state argued strenuously against this change, but the BPR imposed its will by withholding funds. As a consolation, the state paved the loop through Wellston at its own expense, but the loss of mainline traffic permanently stagnated the city's growth.

Three other Oklahoma towns were bypassed in 1932 when the route was removed from Calumet, Geary, and Bridgeport in favor of a direct pathway

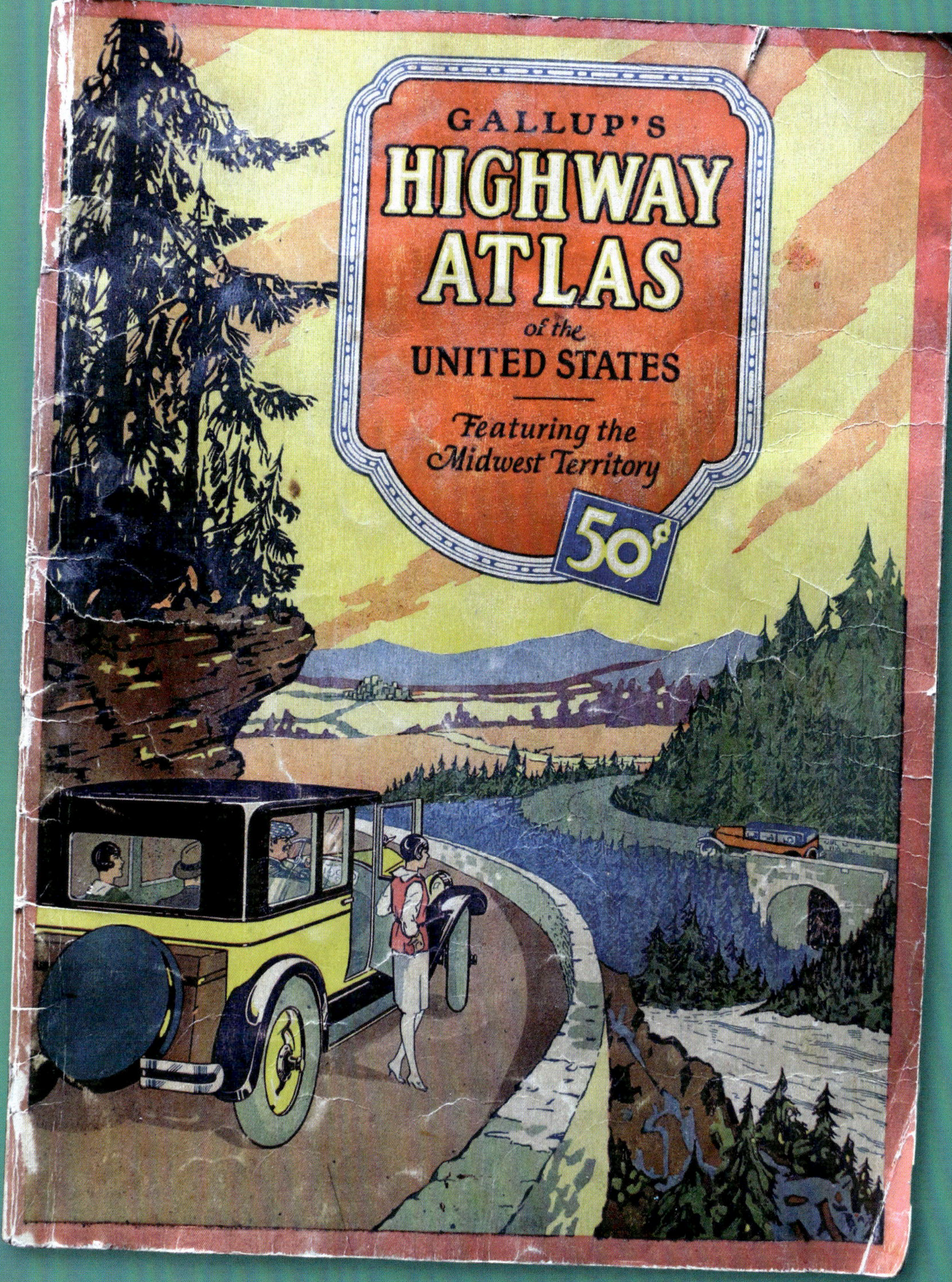

The cover of this 1928 Highway Atlas beckons motorists to hit the road.
Authors' Collection

This metal US 66 highway emblem was used in the early years for promotional purposes. *Kathy Anderson Collection*

The Key suspension bridge carried original US 66 traffic over the South Canadian River at Bridgeport, Oklahoma. *Courtesy of Joel Manning*

from El Reno west to a point just south of Bridgeport. Calumet and Geary remained graced with US 270. Bridgeport, less fortunate, was left isolated and soon became a ghost town.

No state was untouched. In Illinois, US 66 adopted IL 4, which was already paved. But in 1930, as upgrades to the route progressed there, 10 communities on IL 4 were bypassed by a new roadway between Springfield and Staunton several miles to the east. In 1931, the roundabout route through Goffs, California, was redirected, and in 1932 Missouri moved nearly 40 miles of the original route between St. Louis and Gray Summit from Manchester Road to the future path of I-44. The route in New Mexico, including its state capital, was snipped by more than a hundred miles in 1937 when the loop through Santa Fe was eliminated. Important but less significant stretches were bypassed by first-generation paving in Texas and Arizona as well.

Aside from the growing pains, paving projects generated Depression-era jobs and an economic lift to the route's communities. All the while, Americans eagerly awaited the feel of uninterrupted hard surface beneath their wheels. Newspapers praised progress but were quick to criticize delays, even though completion of paving in only 11 years was an exceptional feat by any standard.

The William H. Murray "Pony" Bridge replaced the Key suspension bridge as part of a 1932 bypass. *Courtesy of Shellee Graham*

Early motor courts like Crossman Camp in Texola, Oklahoma, began to appear in the 1920s. *66postcards.com*

Motorists found construction inconveniences a small price to pay. Automobiles now offered more comfort and reliability, motor courts gradually replaced auto camps, and other services improved. When it was done, US 66 emerged as the all-weather gateway to the wonders of the West, and by ambitiously promoting that image, the US Highway 66 Association helped elevate Mother Road tourist traffic well beyond that of other routes.

If not for the 1929 stock market collapse, which left nearly one quarter of America's workforce unemployed, travel-related demand during the decade of paving would have been higher. In the central and southwest states, the struggle worsened in the early 1930s when a merciless drought assailed the land so brutally that homesteaders were driven out. The 1930s would thus be remembered along the route as the decade of both progress and suffering.

California-bound migrants in New Mexico, 1937.
Dorothea Lange, Library of Congress

CHAPTER 4

Hard Times

OT A SINGLE rung of society's pecking order escaped the economic avalanche that slammed the nation on Black Thursday, October 24, 1929. Wealthy investors lost fortunes, suicides spiked, captains of industry slashed production, small businesses closed, and unemployment skyrocketed.

Families everywhere struggled to keep food in the pantry. From the smallest towns to the biggest cities, a generation of self-sufficient and resourceful citizens suddenly found themselves challenged like never before. Government "relief," as it was known, offered little and was something prideful Americans accepted only as a last resort. Any paying job was sought, but for many, especially urbanites, soup lines provided their only opportunity to eat.

Stock market panic on Wall Street, 1929. *National Archives*

America's farms remained viable as long as crops reached harvest, but by the early 1930s severe drought had enveloped the great plains and southwest states. In what was aptly called the "Dust Bowl," fertile fields dehydrated, root systems withered, and loose soil scooped up by whipping winds became blizzards of billowing dust. Without prejudice, the malicious storms randomly dumped millions of tons of airborne soil, leaving drifts across the land. Efforts to keep the grit from invading homes and businesses were futile. Livestock perished and farms were destroyed, entombed under mounds of sand barren as a beach.

A sand drift partially buries this privy on a Cimarron County, Oklahoma, farm in 1936.
Arthur Rothstein, Library of Congress

Farmers succumbed to foreclosure and homelessness. Some were hired as tenants by owners of multiple farms still operating, but in a cruel and ironic twist, many of them and their horse-drawn plows were replaced by tractors their employers bought with government help. Those displaced in this way were "tractored-out," a term heard often during the 1930s. With few resources and fewer prospects, the future for these families was bleak. Most became exiles, forced to flee the blighted states. Help would not come until the Resettlement Administration (later the Farm Security Administration) was operational. By then, the great migration west was several years along. One hanger-on interviewed in Goodlet, Texas, by FSA photographer Dorothea Lange in 1937 had this to say:

"Well, I know I've got to make a move but I don't know where to. I can stay off relief until the first of the year. After that I don't

As disbelieving citizens watch, a massive dust storm invades Elkhart, Kansas, in 1935.
Office of War Information Photograph Collection, Library of Congress

Kids dressed for school use goggles and face wraps during a Lakin, Kansas, dust storm in 1935.
Joyce Unruh, Green Family Collection

know. I've eat up two cows and a pair of horses this year. I've got left two horses and two cows and some farm tools. Owe a grocery bill."

What began as a trickle became an exodus by 1934 as uprooted families gathered their belongings and began the trek to California, where produce jobs were plentiful and the air was fit to breathe. They fled Kansas, Texas, Oklahoma, Arkansas, Colorado, and other states. As John Steinbeck eloquently wrote in *The Grapes of Wrath*, Route 66 became ". . . the Mother Road; the road of flight."

Overloaded clunkers were prone to breakdowns along the way, and as resourceful as they were, without the right parts or money for repairs, migrants had to rely on others equally at risk. Until someone able to help came along, they camped where their vehicles failed. If there was no food, they went hungry.

Arkansas migrants broken down in Oklahoma, 1938.
Dorothea Lange, Library of Congress

"Tractored-out" farmer in Goodlett, Texas, interviewed by Dorothea Lange in 1937.
Dorothea Lange, Library of Congress

In spite of the difficulties, the lure of reaching the "land of milk and honey," as they envisioned it, made the trip a worthwhile gamble. Early arrivals quickly found jobs, but low earnings meant deplorable living conditions and not a penny to spare. Those who followed received a cold reception, and the latecomers who were eventually hired found themselves in the same state of squalor and hopelessness as everyone else. Even as they motored west, families who had waited too long were warned that jobs were scarce. It didn't matter. Without options, most of them trudged on, figuring to beat the odds.

On US 66, diminished tourist traffic left fewer motel rooms occupied, a drop in gallons of gas pumped, and less demand for

The Chandler, Oklahoma, Route 66 Interpretive Center began life as a National Guard Armory built by the WPA in 1936. It stands today as a stellar preservation project. *Courtesy of Shellee Graham*

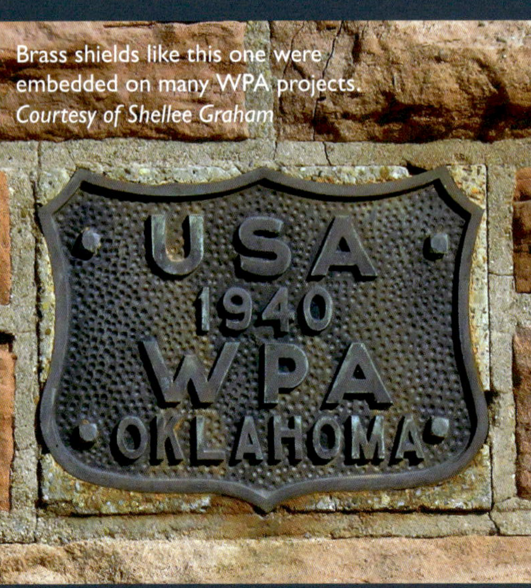

Brass shields like this one were embedded on many WPA projects. *Courtesy of Shellee Graham*

steaming blue-plate specials, even at popular cafés. Roadbuilding jobs brought an economic lift that helped keep dry goods on shelves and greenbacks in cash drawers, but the keepers of the highway also faced the burden of migrants desperate for help. Despite their own struggles, instead of turning their backs, they stepped up, repairing disabled autos or providing enough food or fuel to keep them moving. In return, grateful pilgrims offered to work off their debt. It was a bittersweet fellowship that brought relief to many; even so, hundreds ended up putting down roots wherever their transportation quit or their pockets ran empty. By the late 1930s, close to a half-million families had attempted the journey.

Franklin D. Roosevelt, elected president in 1932, implemented the New Deal recovery and jobs programs. Prominent among them were the Civilian Conservation Corps (CCC) and the Works Progress Administration (WPA). Other New Deal agencies addressed financial reforms, the agricultural crisis, and the tribulations of migrants, but getting them up to speed took time, and they benefitted only a percentage of those in need.

In 1936, author John Steinbeck met Tom Collins, who managed one of the new farm labor camps for the Resettlement Administration. Steinbeck had been commissioned by the *San Francisco News* to write a series of articles about the migrants, and he wanted to see the camps firsthand. The two became fast friends, and through Collins, Steinbeck immersed himself in the migrant world, an odyssey that inspired him to write *The Grapes of Wrath*. His articles for the *News* chronicled the conditions of those who had reached the "land of milk and honey." It was anything but sweet.

The first wave of "Okies" (as most migrants came to be called) who rolled into

California farm country were proud and determined, but had used up everything getting there. They pulled carrots and picked cotton, peas, and all manner of fruit. They were forced to live in "ditch" camps along the roadside or within corporate farm enclaves, where not even water was made available. Wages were skimpy, and workers in some locations were obliged to buy necessities at the company store, where price gouging kept them penniless. Sanitation was virtually nonexistent, as were doctors and medicine, and there was little protection from the elements or the company thugs who wielded clubs to keep order. Missing work due to illness or injury, or inability to keep pace meant no pay or being replaced. Infants and young children died from bacterial infections, measles, flu, mumps, whooping cough, pneumonia, and malnutrition. No measures of prevention were employed and no sympathy given. As non-residents, migrants were not eligible for local or state relief benefits.

By 1936, three job hunters competed for every vacancy. Steinbeck found that 150,000 unemployed migrants were wandering up and down the state. He described them as "that shifting group of nomadic, poverty-stricken harvesters driven by hunger and the threat of hunger, from crop to crop, from harvest to harvest . . ." They were viewed by California residents as a class of dirty, uneducated carriers of disease, and were generally hated. Californians could not see that their own lot would be no different had the migration occurred in the opposite direction. New arrivals were characterized by Steinbeck as "bewildered and beaten and usually in a state of semi-starvation."

Imperial Valley, California migrant camp, 1937. *Dorothea Lange, Library of Congress*

Okie children in a Casa Grande, Arizona, migrant camp, 1937. *Dorothea Lange, Library of Congress*

Pride gave way to survival. Migrants constructed shelters using cardboard, scraps of canvas or sheet metal, discarded

The government-built Kern County, California, migrant camp, 1936.
Dorothea Lange, Library of Congress

plywood, burlap, denim, warped and broken boards, flour sacks, tattered blankets or linens, and whatever else could be scavenged. The camps, according to Steinbeck, from a distance "looked like a city dump."

One song circulating among those marooned in California contained this verse:

I'd rather drink muddy water
Sleep out in a hollow log
Than be in California
*Treated like a dirty dog.**

Attempts to organize or otherwise claw their way out of the sewer they'd landed in were stopped by the political muscle of the Associated Farmers, a powerful consortium of growers and corporate partners. It wasn't until the government camps were built that general welfare improved and dignity was restored. The facilities were sanitary and provided social activities, fundamental health care, and the opportunity for residents to self-govern. They signaled the beginning of the end, but could house only a fraction of the migrant population. The misery endured by the majority would continue until the end of the decade.

Not all migrants traveled as families. Unemployed young men also competed for jobs in California during the Depression era. Those with no transportation or bus fare to get there could buy cheap passage on the "Travel Bureau," an unlawful operation wherein owners of private vehicles hauled passengers for pay. The law considered this unfair competition with bus lines, and if caught, a driver could be jailed and his vehicle confiscated.

In the summer of 1934, 18-year-old Oliver Rooker of Canton, Oklahoma, had one year of high school remaining. He was living with his grandmother, was unemployed, and had only 10 hard-earned dollars stashed in his faded dungarees. After seeing a classified ad he decided to use that money to ride the Travel Bureau to California, unaware he was breaking the law. The westward flow of migrants had by then become a river, and at state-line inspection stations Rooker's group was met with hard questions about their destination and whether the driver had been paid. Rooker had no choice but to join the ruse that they were just friends sharing expenses.

Rooker found only dishwashing jobs in Los Angeles, so he hitch-hiked home, graduated high school in 1935, then booked passage back to L.A., where his luck was no better than before. He returned to Oklahoma and enrolled in college, but a prolonged illness forced him to drop out, so in the spring of 1936 he headed west once again. It was on this trip that he witnessed a flashpoint at a police roadblock that had been set up to turn back all travelers without means.

LAPD Police Chief James Edgar Davis, architect of the "Bum Blockade."
The Cliff Wesselmann Photo Collection, BL Press LLC

The blockade was the brainchild of Los Angeles Police Chief James Edgar Davis, who was motivated by negative public sentiment toward what Californians considered culturally inferior outsiders. Davis's rationale for this overreach was based on proposed legislation inspired by both US and California Supreme Court decisions permitting a state to protect its citizens from "convicts, paupers, idiots and lunatics, and persons likely to become a public charge." The state court also included "sick, diseased, infirm, or disabled persons." In addition, Los Angeles newspapers regularly described Okies as "disease-carrying ne'er-do-wells, 'won't-workers,' and two-legged locusts." **

The California bill to blockade migrants had not yet passed, but that did not deter Chief Davis. He dispatched 136 officers to entry points around the state, many of whom were then deputized by local law enforcement agencies to make it appear legitimate. Supported by public opinion, the press, and by the statehouse, Davis felt justified in his actions.

At an Amarillo Whiting Bros. station, Rooker's group was warned that Los Angeles police had erected a "Bum Blockade" on Route 66 at the California border and that with less than $100 each they would be refused entry into the state. They were warned again leaving New Mexico, but again they pushed on, this time diverting to US 60 where they could enter California at Blythe. Upon arrival there, they found roughly 20 cars pulled over. Los Angeles police with bullhorns barked orders: "California has all the Okies it can take care of. Go back to where you came from.

World War II naval flight crew at an unknown location.
Authors' Collection

You will be arrested if you try to proceed."

It was then that a car pulled up behind them and a big man got out. A policeman approached him, and a shoving match ensued. The officer pulled his gun, and the man was handcuffed, disarmed after a pat-down, and escorted into the guard house. A few minutes later, the mystery man emerged, his firearm returned and handcuffs-free. He grabbed a bullhorn and barked: "Remove that barricade! All you people are free to continue on to your destination! This damn blockade is ended!"

According to Rooker, the big man turned out to be a US Marshal, and he ordered the L.A. police back to their jurisdiction after speaking on the phone with Chief Davis, advising him that his authority to rebuke travelers had no legal standing and violated their rights. By then, growing criticism of the blockades, their cost to the city, and pending lawsuits had already brought pressure to bear, and Chief Davis agreed to stand down.

Rooker fared no better in 1936, but that didn't dissuade him from making a fourth trip to California in 1939. His track record didn't improve. Recently married, he returned home for the last time, completed his education, and had a long career as a journalist, during which he wrote a book about his Travel Bureau exploits.

The Dust Bowl years ended in 1937, but the economic sinkhole from the crash of 1929 lingered. Salvation for Okies stuck in California, when it came, was not from a Wall Street rebound or reforms by growers, but from the acts of Germany and Japan. When the iron fist of war knocked down America's backdoor, unemployment abruptly ended, and the farm collectives in California watched their leverage over migrants vanish like an anvil in quicksand. Suddenly desperate for labor, they reverted to recruiting Mexicans. The ratio of jobs to workers quickly balanced and conditions improved as the Mexicans could simply return home, an escape hatch the migrants never had. The Dust Bowl refugee nightmare was soon mitigated, but not forgotten. It would be remembered as one of the most shameful chapters in American history.

This World War II poster for war bonds was potent and chilling.
National Archives

* * *

On December 7, 1941, the course of humankind was forever altered. Imperial Japan drove a sharp stick into a sleeping bear with its unprovoked attack on the US Fleet at Pearl Harbor, gravely misjudging America's mettle. Growling patriots responded with purpose and vengeance. Europe was already ablaze with bullets; now, in addition to Japan, the United States pursued the emperor's allies in Germany and Italy as well. War was waged globally on multiple fronts with ferocity and without letup until America's enemies were brought to their knees.

Men aged 18 to 45 were eligible for the draft, but nearly 40 percent of the 16 million who served volunteered, eager to retaliate for Pearl Harbor and to stop Germany's quest for world dominance. Americans at home did their part. Women worked in airplane factories and shipyards and munitions plants and fuel depots. They assembled weapons, sewed uniforms, packaged

A US soldier in Europe shares a special moment with a liberated child.
Authors' Collection

Generals George Patton (with pistol), Omar Bradley, and British General Bernard Montgomery in Normandy, France, July 1944.
Morris (Sgt), No 5 Army Film and Photographic Unit, Public Domain, via Wikimedia Common

rations, and manufactured helmets and tanks and parachutes and bombs and medical supplies.

Wartime restrictions placed on liberties were understood and accepted. Mail was censored, and the phrase "loose lips sink ships" became watchwords coast to coast. Citizens bought war bonds, rationed gasoline and food, practiced blackouts, recycled, and planted victory gardens. There was just one egregious overstep—that being the incarceration of more than 100,000 Japanese Americans, rationalized as a protective custody and national security measure. In reality, it was unconstitutional and unnecessary, yet it was upheld by the courts. Admirably, and with few exceptions, Japanese Americans accepted it and remained patriotic throughout their ordeal.

Automotive and other industries switched exclusively to war production. Training bases appeared almost overnight, many of them in California and other locations along America's Main Street. Truck convoys rolled from the industrial centers in the east to military installations in the west, hauling weapons, troops, and

War Dads Canteen, Springfield, Missouri. *Authors' Collection*

New Yorkers celebrate V-J Day in Times Square, 1945. *Library of Congress*

equipment for shipment to the Pacific Theater. In short order, US 66 hummed with activity. Military personnel on leave could hitchhike anywhere with little delay as motorists were eager to show their gratitude. Cafés and gas pumps got busier, and the overall economic upswing elevated morale and helped make withstanding other war-related sacrifices easier. Only the permanent loss and eternal pain of battlefield deaths were insurmountable.

For four years Americans worked feverishly to support the war effort and each other. By the time it was over, fatigue and sorrow had touched virtually every family. Grieving wives and mothers had lost nearly a half-million husbands and sons. A million and a half more returned maimed and injured. And yet their heads were unbowed. When the smoke cleared, celebrating crowds jammed the streets, discharging four years of stress, fear, suspense, and relief in jubilant outpourings of emotion and joy. Every citizen and every surviving soldier had suffered in some way, and had done so with little complaint. They may not have recognized it then, but they truly were the greatest generation.

The Green Book and Threatt Filling Station

"Sundown" towns proliferated during the Jim Crow era of segregation.
Tubman African American Museum, Macon, Georgia

THE SHACKLES of bondage came off when the Civil War ended, but few former slaves were able to capitalize on their freedom. With little or no education and no job opportunities, sharecropping was on the short list of options but offered no future. As time wore on their lot slowly improved, though only within boundaries placed by a society that restricted almost every aspect of their lives. Segregation, job discrimination, and persecution headlined a list of injustices to be overcome. Ratification of the 15th Amendment in 1870 gave African American men the right to vote, but it wasn't until the Civil Rights Act of 1964 that the foundation for meaningful reforms was laid. Prior to that, former slaves and their descendants had been subjected to Jim Crow laws—statutes devised to deny them liberty and keep them oppressed.

By the late 1930s, motoring America's highways was relatively easy, assuming you were not a minority. African Americans were confronted by limited access to restaurants, gas stations, garages, motels, and other businesses. Those that served both races used separate facilities clearly labeled "White" and "Colored." Even more abhorrent, hundreds of

Segregated movie theater in Belzoni, Mississippi, 1939.
Marion Post Walcott, Contributor, Library of Congress

Streetcar Terminal in Oklahoma City, 1939.
Russell Lee, Library of Congress

Cover of the 1956 edition of the Green Book. *Authors' Collection*

Green Book author Victor H. Green. *Public Domain via Wikimedia Commons*

The Threatt Station in Luther, Oklahoma, 1986. *Courtesy of Jerry McClanahan*

towns across the country enacted "sundown" laws, whereby people of color were prohibited within their city limits after dark.

This basket of soiled laundry is not often talked about when telling the Route 66 story. Mark Twain once said that "travel is fatal to prejudice," but such enlightenment was not experienced by non-whites during the Jim Crow era. For them, a road trip equated to navigating a minefield. Venturing out required caution, planning, and often luck to avoid serious trouble.

Another old adage is "Necessity is the mother of invention." So it was that in 1936 a 44-year-old US postal employee named Victor Hugo Green of Harlem, New York, published a travel guide aimed at helping fellow African Americans find places to stay and eat while visiting New York City. *The Negro Travelers' Green Book* quickly proved indispensable, prompting Green to expand its reach to cover the entire country and beyond. Added content included barber shops, filling stations, nightclubs, beauty parlors, repair shops, and more. Except for the war years of the 1940s, the *Green Book* was published annually until 1966, two years after passage of the Civil Rights Act. It was both a testament to the times and a passport for those it was intended to help.

When it comes to the good, bad, and ugly of the route, the *Green Book* harkens to a dark chapter in America's social-cultural maturity. It's an elephant in the room that cannot be ignored. Mr. Green created a counterbalance, one that made travel safer and more enjoyable for those treated so unjustly for so many years. Victor Green died in 1960, but his legacy lives on.

* * *

The reach of the *Green Book* was far and wide, but not every qualifying business was listed. One of those on US 66 in Oklahoma

became so well known that its inclusion wasn't necessary.

In 1920, the family of Allen Threatt Sr. was still new to Oklahoma, having moved from Alabama to the fertile farmland of Wellston, located in Lincoln County. Not long thereafter, Allen and wife Alberta bought from E. J. Canada 160 acres just east of Luther, land that initially had been held out of the final 1895 land run to be leased for funding schools. Their homestead fronted the Ozark Trails, which in 1926 became US 66. In 1933, using stone quarried from their property, the Threatts built the first African American–owned filling station there. Facing the route at the boundary of the Oklahoma–Lincoln County line, the station quickly became known as a friendly stop for people of color. The two-level residential-style structure offered grocery items and had a small café inside, and it later became a state First Aid Station and Greyhound Bus stop.

Allen Threatt Sr.
Courtesy of the Threatt Family

Alberta Threatt.
Courtesy of the Threatt Family

Ulysses Threatt at work at the station.
Courtesy of the Threatt Family

A family of faith, the Threatts instilled values of compassion and honesty in their children. Their land was a color-blind retreat where travelers with no place to stay overnight were welcome to camp on the grounds. On the diamond out back, the crack of bats could be heard whenever Negro League baseball teams came to play, drawing spectators from miles away. During weekend dances hosted by the family, the aroma of saucy barbeque filled the air. Lounging in the shade, elders fanned themselves and sipped sweet tea, recollecting similar gatherings from their youth. In a world where segregation was law, the Threatts provided a comforting, if temporary, reprieve for all to enjoy.

With the passing of Allen Threatt Sr. in 1950, proprietorship was assumed by his son Ulysses and wife Elizabeth. The industrious "Ulyss," as he was called, added a small zoo

The Threatt station in 2024 during its professional restoration. *Courtesy of Shellee Graham*

consisting mainly of a coyote and a racoon. To this he added a snake pit stocked with rattlers he captured on annual hunts. The idea was to attract customers, a draw used to great effect by tourist traps farther west. Ulyss, a World War II veteran, passed away prematurely in 1956, at which time Elizabeth took over. A residence was added to the back of the station for her, where she lived until her passing in 2009 at age 98. In addition to running the station, for half a century Elizabeth was a respected school teacher in Luther, having earned a master's degree in 1959. Her daily routine was to work the café before school, teach her classes, and then return to her duties at the station. This regimen continued until the station finally closed in 1974, when Elizabeth was in her 60s. In recognition of a lifetime of service to the community, the Luther library was renamed in her honor in 2004.

In 1995 the Threatt station was listed on the National Register of Historic Places, and by 2015 descendants of Allen Threatt Sr. had initiated a renovation effort. Grants were awarded from the National Park Service and the National Trust for Historic Preservation. Other fundraisers followed, and the building was professionally restored. Now a landmark visitor's stop, the Threatt station's rich history is shared by the family who has immeasurably served their community as well as Mother Road travelers for nearly 100 years.

The accomplished Elizabeth Hilton Threatt. *Courtesy of the Threatt Family*

C. David Threatt and Edward Threatt Sr., grandsons of Allen Threatt Sr., managed the restoration effort. (Pictured here with author Shellee Graham.) *Courtesy of Jim Ross*

Chief Wolf Robe Hunt (far right) and family
at the Smithsonian Institution in 1928.
National Anthropological Archives, Smithsonian Institution

CHAPTER 5

The Mother Road Meets Native America

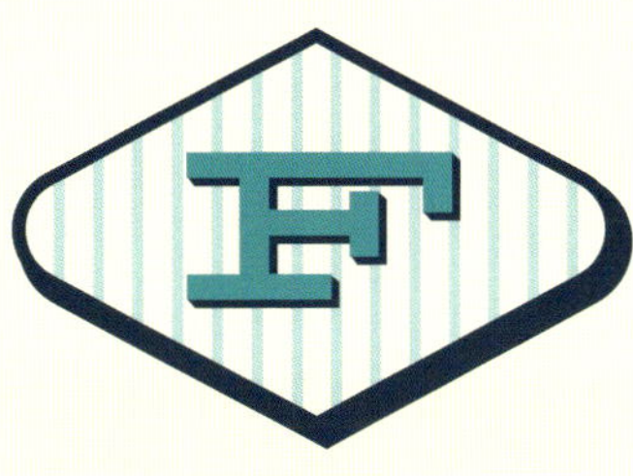

RED HARVEY built an empire in partnership with the Santa Fe Railroad, first providing food service in dining cars and at their depots across the West and then designing and operating elaborate hotels for their passengers, all featuring his impeccable restaurants. These became known as "Harvey Houses" and included locations along US 66 as well as at the Grand Canyon and elsewhere.

Prior to the widespread use of automobiles, tourists arriving by rail in Albuquerque, New Mexico, were introduced to Native American art at Harvey's sprawling Alvarado Hotel. Opened in 1902, it featured both a museum (the "Indian Building") and an outdoor area where tribal artisans displayed and sold their crafts. Harvey later advanced this mingling of cultures with the creation of the "Indian Detours," headquartered in Santa Fe's La Fonda Hotel on the route's pending first alignment.

Fred Harvey, founder of Harvey House hotels and restaurants. *Kansas Historical Society via Wikipedia*

Tourists interact with Native American artisans outside the Indian Building at Albuquerque's Alvarado Hotel in 1920. *Keystone View Company, Library of Congress*

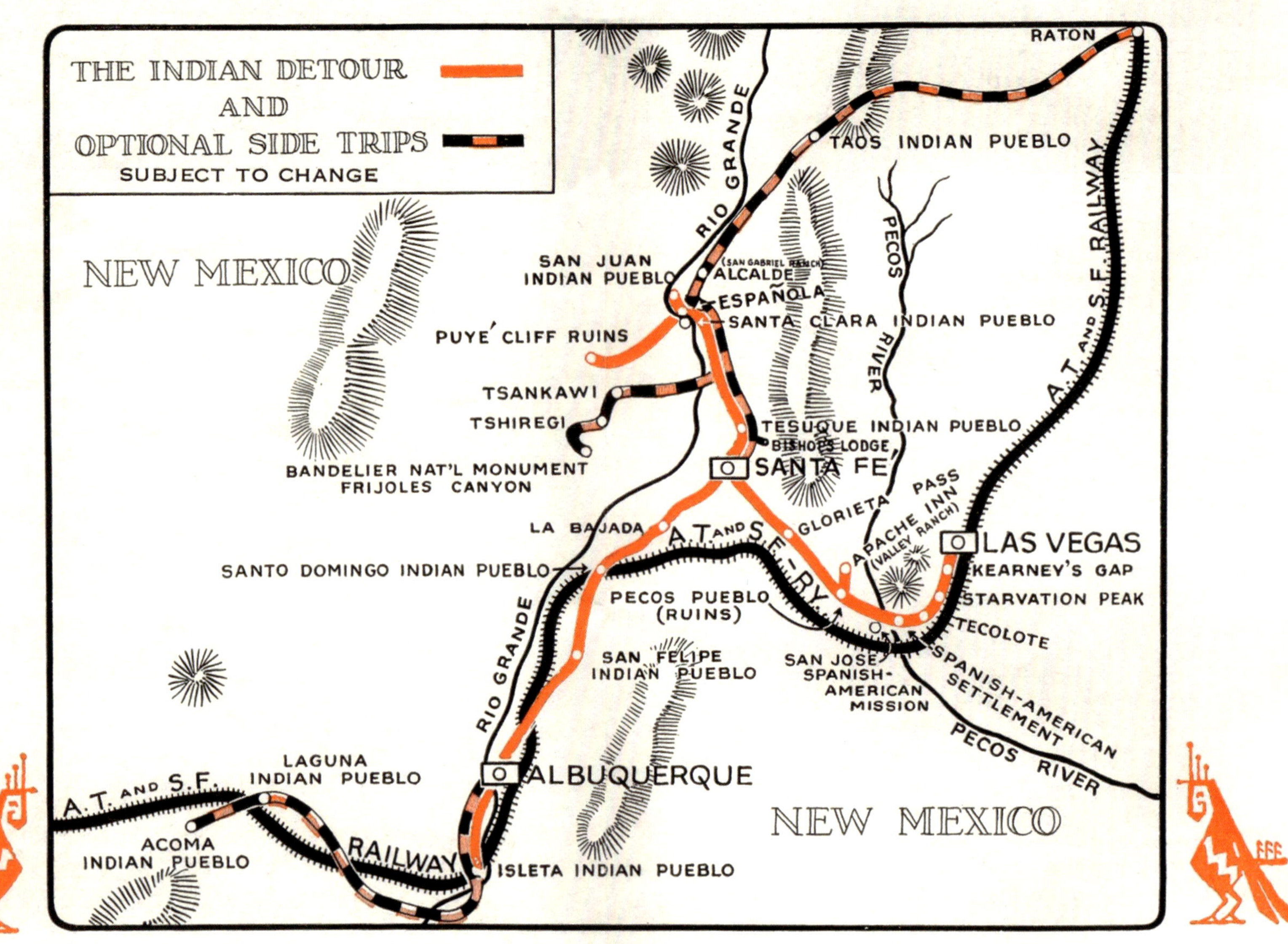

An Indian Detours map for tourists, from a 1927 brochure. *Authors' Collection*

It was Harvey Company chief of transportation, R. Hunter Clarkson, who conceived the idea of shuttling tourists to Indian pueblos in the region. The tours premiered in 1926, offering three-day outings at $45 per person from hubs in Santa Fe, Las Vegas, and Albuquerque. Participants were chauffeured in Packards and Cadillacs by attractive women dubbed "Couriers," and luxury buses from the White Motor Company were used for the tours. Destinations on Route 66 included Santo Domingo, San Felipe, Isleta, and Laguna.

By the late 1930s, autos had surpassed trains as the primary mode of travel, and with their source of customers steadily depleting, the Indian Detours were discontinued. Though relatively short-lived,

Interior of a luxury White Motor Coach used for Indian Detours.
Authors' Collection

Indian Detours passengers visit San Juan Pueblo, north of Santa Fe.
Authors' Collection

The original Hubbell Trading Post at Ganado, Arizona.
Courtesy of Shellee Graham

they played a supporting role in the merging of Native American and Anglo commercialism and strengthened cultural interactions across the Southwest.

Indian trading posts had existed since the days of fur trappers and buffalo hunters. They sold or traded to tribal members animal hides, tobacco, alcohol, horses, and guns in exchange for jewelry, rugs, and pottery. Toward the end of the 19th century, with the buffalo herds nearly destroyed, a new generation of traders stocked dry goods and other industrialized items to help fill the gap. By then, most Native Americans were on their respective reservations. One of those traders was John Lorenzo Hubbell, who set up shop on the Navajo reservation in 1878 at Ganado, Arizona, soon after the Navajo returned from five years of exile at the Bosque Redondo reservation near Ft. Sumner, New Mexico.

John Lorenzo Hubbell, circa 1920.
National Park Service-Hubbell Trading Post

With his sons, Hubbell eventually owned more than 20 trading posts as well as freight and stage lines. His original Ganado location remained in family hands until its transfer to the National Park Service in 1967. Now a National Historic Site, it is located less than 40 miles north of the route from Chambers, where it continues to serve both tourists and tribal members under management of the nonprofit Western National Parks Association. The building for Hubbell's Winslow, Arizona, location still stands as well and is now a visitor center.

By the 1920s, trading posts such as Richardson's in Gallup catered to tourists in urban settings, and within a decade the

Plaza in Santa Fe became a premier location for tribal artisans to offer their wares in an open-air setting. The city of Gallup, New Mexico, hosted its first Inter-Tribal Indian Ceremonial festival in 1922, featuring dancers, a parade, and a rodeo, with nearly a dozen regional tribes represented. The Ceremonial has been repeated every year since and has become one of New Mexico's longest-standing and most important events, with more than 50 tribes participating.

Native Americans welcomed and benefitted from the economic uplift brought by US 66. They willingly shared their culture with tourists, to include wearing ceremonial dress. Most tribes viewed this theatrical aspect simply as doing business; like the Gallup event, it allowed them to expose their heritage and art to a wider audience.

Interplay was not limited to artisans and tourists. The traditional lifestyle of Native Americans helped insulate them from the effects of the Great Depression and Dust Bowl. Famed photographer and Laguna Indian Lee Marmon was raised in Laguna, New Mexico, and as a young boy witnessed the plight of the Dust Bowl migrants. He spoke of it in his book *Laguna Pueblo: A Photographic History*, describing acts of compassion by tribal residents:

Inter-Tribal Ceremonial program cover from the 1938 event.
Authors' Collection

Dine' Navajo dancers Calvert Dixon and Bennie Yazzie at an event in Holbrook, Arizona, in 2023.
Used with permission, photo by John Gerald Jimenez

Native Americans parade through Gallup, New Mexico, during the Inter-Tribal Ceremonial.
Authors' Collection

Post office and store, Laguna, New Mexico, circa 1930. *Steve Rider Collection*

Renowned photographer Lee Marmon of Laguna, New Mexico. *Courtesy of Kathryn Marmon*

"They came . . . in old jalopies with all their kids, and grandma or grandpa, along with their dog or cat—even chickens. They would pass through Laguna with no food and no money, and they would be running out of gas. They were proud, never asking for a handout. Sometimes local people would give them enough gas to get to Grants.

"My grandpa Jack Stagner and uncle Grover Stagner built an auto camp on the Marmon compound. Many of the people were destitute. Some were sick. One night we heard screams from the auto camp. A woman was having a baby and then it died. We buried it in the next yard where my grandfather was buried, and the family moved on."

Such heartfelt expressions of humanity were not confined to Laguna. Migrants received help with fuel, food, money, and auto repairs from tribal communities

Claude Bowlin's original Old Crater Trading Post near Bluewater, New Mexico. Note the rug weaver at work, left side of photo.
Authors' Collection

across New Mexico and Arizona. Like elsewhere along the route, these gestures enabled many to complete their pilgrimage, for better or worse.

* * *

By the time paving was completed in 1938, most trading posts had wandered from their traditional purpose, paying tribal customers in cash or store credit in exchange for jewelry and other crafts. Yet they remained a key link between Native America and the world outside their reservations. In urban settings, the more prominent locations employed silversmiths in-house. Elsewhere, the majority sold gas and stocked sundry items in addition to tribal offerings. Novelty items and souvenirs, best described as "curios," found their way onto trading post shelves as vacation traffic increased, and they proved popular with tourists looking for inexpensive items. Individual curio shops, located mostly in town business districts, also found their niche along the route. At this point, few tourists traveling out west ended their trip without having encountered Native American culture to some degree.

Claude T. Bowlin's Old Crater Trading Post near Bluewater, New Mexico, was by then a rarity. Bowlin, who built the trading post in 1936, traded with local Navajo and sold only authentic

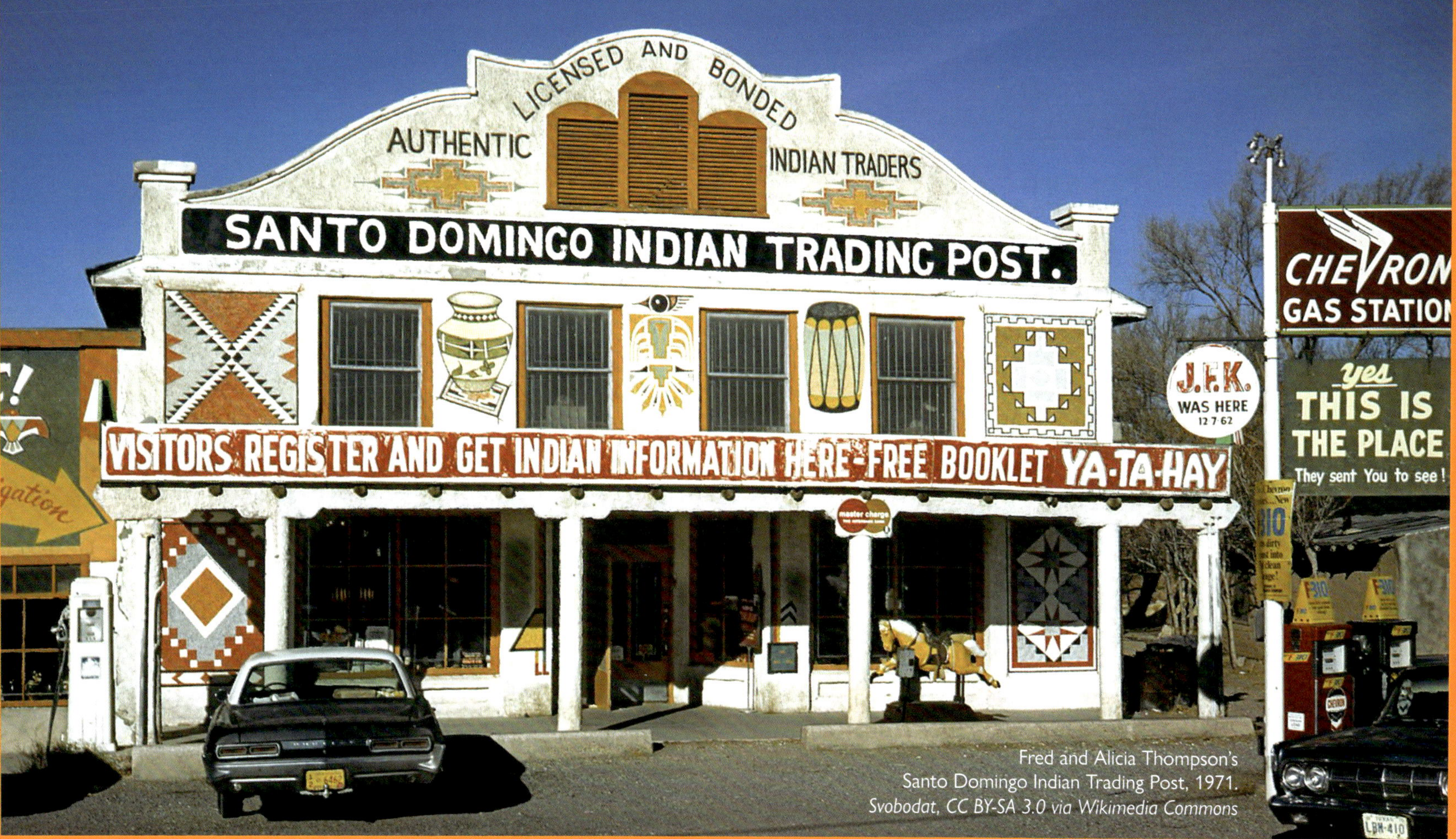

Fred and Alicia Thompson's
Santo Domingo Indian Trading Post, 1971.
Svobodat, CC BY-SA 3.0 via Wikimedia Commons

Native American goods. He also educated tourists on how to distinguish genuine from replica jewelry and was a member of the United Indian Traders Association. Bowlin replaced the post's original building in 1954. Twenty years later it closed permanently following its 1973 bypass by Interstate 40. It is now a roadside ruin.

Another was the Santo Domingo Indian Trading Post located on the route southwest of Santa Fe, New Mexico. Built in 1922 by the Seligman family at the site of a small, 1800s trading post, the 4,400-square-foot Mission Revival–style adobe building was located just two miles east of the Santo Domingo-Kewa Pueblo. Originally named Wallace for New Mexico territorial governor Lew Wallace (Wallace became famous as the author of *Ben-Hur*), Domingo was a railway stop for travelers between Santa Fe and Albuquerque and a hub for area pueblos. Business was such that at its peak the Seligmans had more than 20 employees.

The dirt road in front of the trading post was US 66 from 1926 until it was moved to the east and paved in 1932. Business then stagnated, and the Seligmans sold out to Mike Leyva, who relied on railway passengers to keep it breathing for the next 17 years. In 1949 it was acquired by "Trader" Fred Thompson, a colorful character who made the trading post internationally known through a campaign of national advertising and old-fashioned salesmanship.

The Bell Trading Post at 403 W. Copper in Albuquerque. *Contributed by Alabama Milner, Albuquerque Museum*

Thompson, born in 1909 in Rochester, New York, met his wife, Alicia Montoya, in the 1940s when he was an Army sergeant stationed at Camp Luna, New Mexico, and she was a nurse at Bruns Army Hospital in Santa Fe. Following duty in the China-Burma theater, Fred returned to New Mexico, where the two married in 1946. They settled in Rochester, but not for long. Frequent vacations to Alicia's New Mexico birthplace of Pena Blanca enticed Fred to buy the Santo Domingo trading post, and in 1950 they returned permanently to New Mexico. Fred often joked to visitors that he came there from New York "as a male war bride."

The Thompsons traded dry goods, clothing, and other staples to the residents of pueblos throughout the region in exchange for handmade jewelry, beadwork, rugs, and pottery. They enjoyed success for more than 40 years, when their energy finally waned due to advancing age and family tragedy. In 1993, Alicia and Fred's only son, George, died on a motorcycle at the hands of a drunk driver in Santa Fe. By then, with Fred 83 and Alicia 80, shelves were largely bare, and the few customers who wandered in were met only by the sounds of creaky floors and the whir of ceiling fans stirring stale air. In 1994, Fred died of a heart attack. Alicia joined him in 1996. The two are buried side by side in the Santa Fe National Cemetery.

The Santo Domingo Trading Post, added to the National Register of Historic Places in 1998, was gutted by fire in 2001. Six years later, the National Park Service approved a stabilization grant, and in 2011 it began rising from the rubble thanks to additional grants obtained by the Santo Domingo-Kewa tribe. These efforts have preserved both the storied history of the trading post and, fittingly, the legacy and contributions of Fred and Alicia Thompson.

Staff artisans pose at Maisel's original Albuquerque location in 1935. *Albuquerque Museum, gift of Norman Maisel*

Richardson's Trading Post in Gallup, New Mexico. *Courtesy of Jim Ross*

Maisel's on Central Avenue circa 1945. *Albuquerque Museum, gift of Jeff McDaniel*

Interior view of Maisel's in 1953. *Albuquerque Museum, gift of Norman Maisel*

During the pre-interstate years, other trading posts enjoyed similar success but in urban settings. Two of them were Maisel's and the Bell Trading Post, both in Albuquerque. Located at Fourth and Copper on the original route, Bell was opened in 1932 by Jack and Mildred Michelson using Mildred's maiden name. They had little competition until 1939, when Austrian immigrant Maurice Maisel moved from his original store on South First Street to 510 Central Avenue following the relocation of US 66. Both had Indian artisans in-house and bought from hundreds of others.

Following Michelson's 1957 death, ownership passed to his three children, whose primary focus became wholesale distribution. In 1969 they changed their brand to Sunbell and remained active until the late 1980s. Maisel's had closed in 1968 following Maurice's death but was reopened in 1985 by his grandson Skip. Maisel's continued as a premier trading post until closing permanently when Skip retired in 2019.

All the while, Richardson Trading Company in Gallup has progressed seamlessly into the route's second century. The granddaddy of Route 66 survivors, its origins date back to 1913 when Claude Richardson and his brother Hubert opened a store to serve the Navajo and Hopi reservations in northeast Arizona. Within a few years they relocated to Winslow to open a wholesale house. Claude established a downtown Gallup trading post in the mid-1930s, and in 1939 Richardson's present location opened under the management of Claude's son Bill and wife Mattie.

Bill's stewardship continued until his death in 2017 at age 98. He and Mattie's old-school manner of doing business was a family hallmark, and it shows. Richardson's expansive interior contains endless glass cases crowded with sparkling jewelry of every type and price range. Aisles of Native American products beckon browsers. Rugs hang like drapes above rows of saddles and racks of rifles. Dancing kachinas frozen in time occupy tiers of shelving. The vast menagerie of Indian relics and regalia gives the spacious building the feel of a hushed museum where everything except the stuffed buffalo is for sale.

Interior view of Richardson's Trading Post.
Courtesy of the Richardson Family

* * *

Countless silversmiths and other Indian artisans populated the Route 66 corridor. Many of them became nationally known, such as Navajo silversmith Kenneth Begay, Hopi artist Fred Kabotie, and San Ildefonso potter Maria Montoya Martinez. Accomplished Indian entrepreneurs were not in short supply, either. A few of these, such as Mescalero Apache Joe Deer Foot, were Indian chiefs whose achievements went far beyond merchandising.

The Deer Foot Trading Post east of downtown Gallup, New Mexico, pulsed with personality. Chief Joe Deer Foot was born on May 6, 1889, at Fort Sill, Oklahoma, during the time of Geronimo's imprisonment there. Information about his path to adulthood is sketchy, as he was orphaned by the death of his father while still a boy. After time spent in a Nebraska foster home, he rambled

Navajo silversmith Kenneth Begay, circa 1946.
Leslie Kee Photo Collection

San Ildefonso potter Maria Martinez.
Courtesy of AntiqueAmericanIndianArt.com

Hopi artist Fred Kabotie in 1932.
Grand Canyon National Park, CC by 2.0 via Wikimedia Commons

Chief Joe Deer Foot on his trick horse, Bob Burns. *Kansasmemory.org, Kansas State Historical Society*

Chief Deer Foot (far left) at his trading post in Gallup, New Mexico, 1955. *Authors' Collection*

around the West before serving in World War I. Joe became an expert horseman and archer, and following the war built a name for himself performing bullwhip, archery, and trick-riding exhibitions in full Indian dress at fairs and circuses. This led to his only movie role, a major part in the 1924 silent film *North of Nevada*, a shoot-'em-up western in which he played an outlaw Indian out to snatch water rights from greenhorn ranchers.

In 1939, Joe married Ora Norton in Brooks, Texas, and they settled in Gallup, where Joe opened the trading post and continued making regional appearances. He toured Europe, "performing feats of horsemanship," and regularly rode at the head of Gallup's Inter-Tribal Ceremonial parade on his horse Bob Burns, a pinto that could count, climb stairs, and drink soda pop from a bottle. Known for his sense of humor and flair for storytelling, Joe was asked by Gallup officials in 1948 to greet President Harry Truman during a whistlestop there. When they met, Chief Deer Foot presented the president with an authentic Indian rug and war bonnet and pronounced him an honorary chief.

President Truman accepts a rug from Chief Joe Deer Foot in Gallup, New Mexico, June 15, 1948. *Harry S. Truman Library and Museum, National Archives*

Chief Joe loved his Indian heritage and loved his country. He passed away, notably, on July 4, 1966, at age 77. Ora, 21 years younger, survived him until 2001. Close friend Bill Richardson proudly accepted Joe's buckskin outfit and war bonnet for display at Richardson's store, where they remain today.

* * *

Acoma Chief Henry Wolf Robe Hunt was 23 years old when he stood stoically for a family portrait taken at the Smithsonian Institution in 1928. His father, Chief Day Break, was

Wolf Robe Hunt's Indian Trading Post on Route 66 in Tulsa, Oklahoma. The building was demolished in 1998. *Courtesy Tulsa Historical Society and Museum*

there to record Acoma history, which museum curators translated from his native language. While young Henry took such tribal duties seriously, he nurtured a passion for art, dance, and mentoring youngsters as well.

Born Wayne Henry Hunt at the Acoma Pueblo in 1905 to Morning Star and Chief Day Break (Edward Proctor Hunt), Henry assumed the name "Wolf Robe" from a Cheyenne chief of the same name. A quick study, he learned silversmithing from his older brother and was already active in Indian dance by the time he graduated high school in Albuquerque, after which he enrolled at the University of New Mexico. There, he studied art under famed artist Carl Redin.

Henry married Glenal Davis in 1933, and they relocated to Tulsa, Oklahoma, where Henry continued his studies under artist and educator Frank von der Lancken and opened Wolf Robe's Indian Trading Post on the route's 11th Street alignment near downtown. As his reputation as an artisan grew, he also became known for advocating improved inter-tribal relations and for mentoring Boy Scouts in Native American dance.

Wolf Robe Hunt's brother-in-law was zoologist Hugh Davis of nearby Catoosa. In 1959, the two partnered to open the Catoosa Indian Trading Post (later

Arrowood) on Hugh's Route 66 frontage there. It was Hugh Davis who constructed the Blue Whale complex just across the highway from the trading post in the early 1970s—a family project destined to evolve into one of the route's most beloved icons.

One of Henry's most treasured honors was performing "The Rite of the Last Arrow" for oil man, Indian art collector, philanthropist, and museum founder Thomas Gilcrease of Tulsa, who was part Creek Indian and a close friend of Hunt. The sacred Indian burial ritual is highlighted by the firing of an arrow pointed at the setting sun, which Hunt carried out on the museum grounds following Gilcrease's passing in 1962.

Postcard portrait of Chief Wolf Robe Hunt.
Authors' Collection

A silver and turquoise brooch by Wolf Robe Hunt.
Authors' Collection

Throughout the decade, Henry traveled Europe, representing the American Indian for the Department of Agriculture. By then he had become a nationally recognized tribal ambassador, artist, author, sculptor, silversmith, and dance troupe leader who produced museum-quality work. He was a skilled illustrator, lecturer, and leader of the Acoma Snake Dancers, and in 1973 was named Oklahoma's Indian of the Year.

Henry Wolf Robe Hunt led an extraordinary life. On December 10, 1977, he passed away at age 72, leaving behind a legacy of art and teaching that will endure for generations.

Laguna tribal member Tzu-chey poses at the pueblo in 1902.
Henry G. Peabody, Library of Congress

* * *

Native American culture represents a sizeable slice of the Route 66 pie and always has. Imagine the route with no artisans populating Santa Fe's Plaza. Imagine no pueblos along the route, no teepees, no trading posts, and no jewelry or pottery or kachinas or rugs. Imagine no souvenir moccasins or tomahawks or replica war bonnets. Imagine not a single neon sign featuring an Indian chief or related symbol. Imagine the patina of the Mother Road without the brush strokes of Native America.

Postcard Messages from the Road

SINCE THE 1870S, postcards have helped those on the road share the journey with the home folks. They allow travelers to export their experiences, document progress, and report mishaps. Some vacationers buy spares as mementos or mail them to their home address. Postmarks indelibly record the date and location from where a card was mailed, often revealing a subsequent stop and the distance from the point of purchase, not unlike a tracking device. For merchants, postcards pay for themselves when purchased, and then become advertisements after they leave the lot. Historians use them to verify locations and timelines. Messages might be informative, revealing, funny, or harken to an era or event. Most are simply sent as a greeting from the road or a promise kept.

Gallup, New Mexico ▲

Dear Bob, How would you like some clothes like this? People who dressed this way still do—in Gallup, New Mex., where I'm staying tonight. It's chock full of Injuns! But all they want is my money—not my scalp. Love, Aunt Mil *(Mailed circa 1959 from Gallup, New Mexico, to Van Nuys, California).*

La Bajada Mesa, New Mexico (1932 Upgrade Alignment) ▲

Dear Mother: This is a picture of the new highway down this hill. You and Letha will probably remember the 23 hairpin turns of 1926. The old Hudson just barely made them. We are enjoying our trip. Stayed here in Albuquerque last night. Love, Kent & Velda *(Postmarked September 17, 1962, in Albuquerque, New Mexico, and mailed to Kingman, Kansas).*

Hotel Jefferson, St. Louis, Missouri ▲

Hello Darling: This will give you my new address and I want to hear from you more often. I will write a letter later. How about sending me a picture of yourself in a small soldiers picture folder. Would appreciate it very much. How have you been, swell I hope. Sure wish I could be with you for awhile. I rather miss good ole LA. There is nothing here that will compare with it. Please write real often. Yours, Harvey. (*Postmarked May 3, 1942. Mailed free of postage from Ft. Benning, Georgia, to Los Angeles. The sender was Candidate H. E. Mahling, 21st Company, 8th Battalion, 2nd Student Training Regiment. Likely sent near the end of his officer training. Note: Harvey Mahling became an infantry officer. He survived the war and retired as a lieutenant colonel. He passed away in 1966 at age 51*).

Painted Desert, Arizona ➤

Mon. Eve—St. Louis. Hi, just wrote you a gripe letter, then went outside the motel—Bob in a hammock, me in an easy chair—and the heat all gone—wonderful breeze, lots of lightning, a fascinating display, and a little thunder. Hope it really means a blessed rain. Haven't seen lightning like this for 30 years. Love, Mother. P.S. Did you mail our checks for bills? *(Postmarked June 18, 1952, in St. Louis, Missouri, and mailed to San Bernardino, California).*

Premier Motel, Albuquerque, New Mexico ▲

10-11-56 Hi: Staying at this motel tonight. Had another wonderful day. Saw some deer when we started out this AM. Stopped in several Indian Trading Posts today. Saw lots of Indians and their hogans (huts). Went through Petrified Forest and Painted Desert today. Both beautiful. Really heading east again now. Love Vi. *(Postmarked October 12, 1956, in Albuquerque, New Mexico, and mailed to South Portland, Maine).*

DETOUR

Lava Beds, Near Grants, New Mexico ▲

Dear John (and TEAM!) Left Tuesday afternoon and drove straight through to Amarillo in 30 hours. God! Car and trailer doing fine, however, had to get a new fuel pump ($10) when the car stopped—50 yards from the only garage within 70 miles! "Somebody up there . . . etc." Bought some really fine Indian pottery for a song—will try to drive straight thru to L.A. from here—700 miles. Keep humping. Ian Thurs. A.M. *(Postmarked September 4, 1959, in Gallup, New Mexico, and mailed to Ohio State University in Columbus).*

Street View, Shamrock, Texas ▲

Kum Kwick as you can. Don *(Postmarked February 5, 1958, in Amarillo, Texas, and mailed to Webster, New York).*

Trails Arch Bridge, Arizona / California State Line ➤

Thursday Morning Topock, Arizona. Dear Folks, got here at 9:10 and have to wait until 11:00—they are repairing this big bridge & you can only cross at 9 – 11 – & 4 & we missed it by ten minutes—so we have had our oil drained—filled with gas & are now drinking coffee & eating sandwiches. Love, Mart, Robert & Marian *(Postmarked January 12, 1929, in Topock, Arizona, and mailed to Atwood, Kansas).*

COLORADO RIVER BRIDGE, TOPOCK, ARIZONA

War Dad's Canteen, Springfield, Missouri ▲

A1C Vernon L. Light 16018926 I-3 Box 34, Maxwell Field, Ala. Hello Honey—it's 6:00 Friday nite and we just got to Springfield, MO. Train sure is dirty. We all look like pigs. L & K VLL *(Postmarked May 25, 1945, as free mail via the Railway Mail Service (RMS) at the STL & Monett Railroad Post Office, Train 4, and mailed to Neuman, Illinois. Note: Airman First Class Vernon Light became a chief warrant officer. He passed away at age 86 on Christmas Day 2009).*

Greetings from St. Louis, Missouri ▲

Hi Folks, I'm really seeing some country and getting over some ground. This is off the record but right now I'm sharing a seat with a swell looking sailor. Love, Elenora *(Postmarked August 31, 1944, in Pecos, Texas, and mailed to Leavittsburg, Ohio).*

Cactus Motor Lodge, Tucumcari, New Mexico ►

Hello, Sat. Nite. This is where we are staying tonite, the loveliest motor court you ever saw. We 4 have a double cottage, steam heated, door open between 2 rooms. So nice having a regular little home. It's so attractive both inside and outside. Lovely furniture, hard wood floors with Indian rugs on them. Tiled baths in each room. We go to Santa Fe N.M. tomorrow to visit friends of folks. Also have radio in each room. Surely having a lovely trip. Lots of snow here. Love, Marie *(Postmarked February 3, 1948, in Tucumcari, New Mexico, and mailed to Williamsville, Illinois).*

Albuquerque's Central Avenue is a dazzling spectacle in this 1953 photo, even in black and white. Note the Alvarado Hotel sign at left center. *Albuquerque Museum, Gift of Albuquerque National Bank*

CHAPTER 6

Get Your Kicks

Occupants of a 1947 Pontiac sedan with a window-mounted swamp cooler visit the Petrified Log Station just off the route in Holbrook, Arizona.
Authors' Collection

HE PAIN INFLICTED during the Depression and war years was like brass knuckles to the teeth, but it didn't stop those with means from traveling, whether for business or pleasure. Family vacations had been fewer, but no less memorable. Throughout the 1930s, autos became more reliable and could reach point B from point A more quickly and with fewer breakdowns. For the most part, conditioning the air was still achieved by rolling down windows, and gas mileage was poor, but these were not deterrents. In 1946, with the war over and gas rationing lifted, automotive plants resumed churning out new models for those eager to see the America they had fought so valiantly to save. New beginnings illuminated the horizon, and post-war euphoria unleashed traffic in a flash flood.

V-J Day was the linchpin to the future, and the future streaked in like an escaped comet. The war's end opened endless doors. The ugliness of the past had been vanquished; all eyes anticipated tomorrow's rewards. It was the eve of the space age courtesy of jet propulsion and rocket science. The sky was the limit.

Experimental rocket launch at Cape Canaveral, Florida, in 1948.
Courtesy of NASA

In this ad for the 1946 Ford, "Let's Go!" perfectly describes the enthusiasm Americans had for road trips following the war.
Authors' Collection

Palo Duro Canyon, just south of Amarillo, Texas, is the second largest in the United States. *Courtesy of Jim Livingston*

Initially ignored was the Cold War, which loomed like a boogeyman in the closet but had yet to cast its frightful net. With the war in the rearview mirror, Americans paused just long enough to mourn the dead, lick their wounds, and draw a deep breath. They were free and they were grateful. America's Main Street, already ripe with history, switched its conductor's hat from the road of flight to the vacation highway. Wonders of the West such as Palo Duro Canyon, the Petrified Forest, Meteor Crater, the Grand Canyon, and star-studded Hollywood stood waiting like pop-up targets.

A vacationing family pauses for a roadside lunch. *Authors' Collection*

Colorful downtown Albuquerque in the 1940s.
Authors' Collection

Bobby and Cynthia Troup on their wedding day in 1942.
Courtesy of the Troup Family Archives

From the hardware store to the service garages, cafés, and motels, the pace quickened. Prosperity spread like jelly on toast. Motor courts outfitted with wall heaters, cramped bathrooms, and coin-operated radios would soon give way to those with air conditioning, televisions, and swimming pools. No longer would weary travelers roll into a darkened town at the end of a long day thanks to neon-saturated boulevards that beckoned like silent carnival barkers from miles away. Soldiers by the thousands had trained at bases in the West, and visiting places they couldn't at the time was now as easy as putting their wheels on US 66.

Recently discharged Marine Corps Captain Bobby Troup was one of them. Born in 1918, he attended the Wharton School of Business, and while there composed a jazzy tune called "Daddy" for a 1937 school production. The song became popular and was recorded by the Sammy Kaye Band in 1941. It was a hit, earning Troup a job in New York writing for Tommy Dorsey and Harry James. In the spring of 1942, he enlisted in the Marine Corps, married dancer Cynthia Hare, and had another of his songs, "Snootie Little Cutie," recorded by Frank Sinatra and Connie Hines with the Tommy Dorsey Orchestra.

Troup attended officer training and was then assigned to the Black Marine recruit depot at Montford Point, North Carolina. While there, he assembled the first African American Marine Corps band and continued composing songs. After deployment to Saipan in 1944, he was discharged and returned to his home in Lancaster, Pennsylvania, but only long enough to finalize plans for a move to Los Angeles. "Daddy" had earned him enough to buy a snazzy Buick convertible, and in February 1946 he and Cynthia motored west.

Prior to connecting with US 66 in St. Louis, Cynthia suggested writing a song about the highway they were on, Route 40. Bobby was intrigued, but preferred they wait until they were on US 66, their primary route to California. Once on the Mother Road, Cynthia began rhyming town names on the map. It suddenly came to her, and she excitedly whispered to Bobby, "Get your kicks on Route 66." Bobby's response was an immediate "Yes!" and they began composing lyrics for the first verse.

Once in Los Angeles, Troup sought an introduction through his New York contacts to crooner Nat King Cole, who performed Troup's type of jazz. Cole liked what he heard and asked Bobby to finish it for an upcoming recording session. "Get Your Kicks on Route 66" was a smash hit for the King Cole Trio and ultimately became the anthem of the highway. Bobby Troup went on to a successful career as a composer, singer, and actor.

Geographer Arthur Krim reveals in *Route 66: Iconography of the American Highway* that Bobby Troup's hit song was significant in other ways. His decision to stick with his homespun dialect caused a change in the common pronunciation of the word "route," which in the northeast was pronounced "root." Most everywhere else it was "rowt." Over time, "root" became the popular pronunciation due to the song. Krim explains that Troup also expanded the route's symbolism by avoiding the more common term "Highway 66," as used by Steinbeck and others during the Depression and Dust Bowl years. By using "Route 66," Troup cast a view of the road as more of a tourist highway than a road of flight, bringing a subtle but lasting shift in identity.

* * *

Bobby Troup wasn't alone in making his mark in 1946. The same year, a 33-year-old Californian named Jack D. Rittenhouse foresaw the need for something meatier than a map for traveling the route. The result was *A Guidebook to Highway 66*, which he self-published following a road trip to collect material. The book contained strip maps and data about the communities, along with landmarks, road conditions, lodging, and other services. Also included were distances between towns and points of interest. A typical entry (from Illinois) reads:

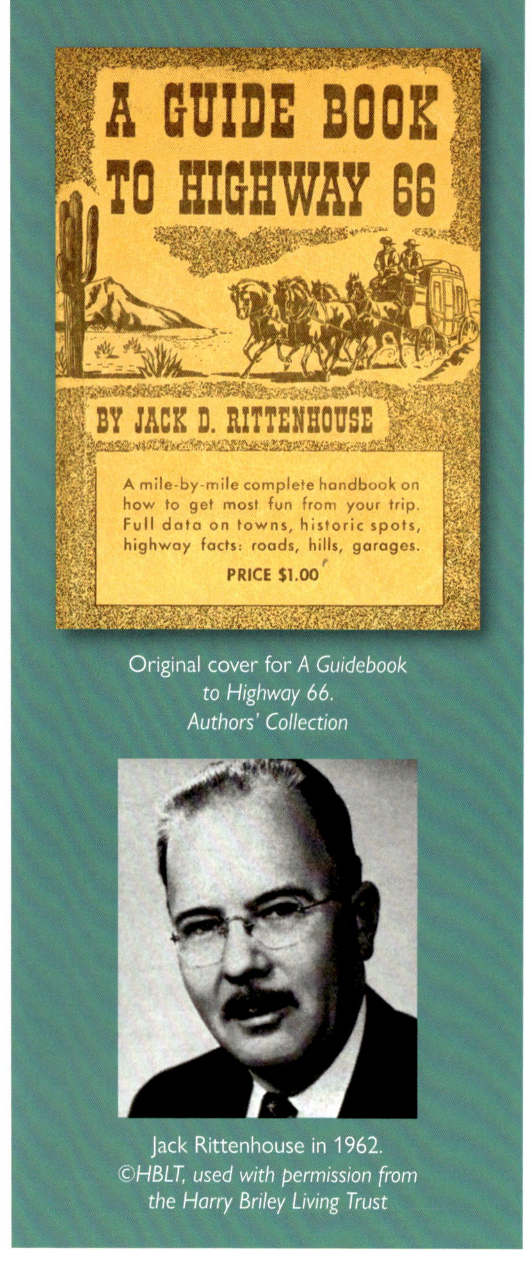

Original cover for *A Guidebook to Highway 66.*
Authors' Collection

Jack Rittenhouse in 1962.
©HBLT, used with permission from the Harry Briley Living Trust

"67 mi. (179 mi.) CHENOA. (Pop. 1401; alt. 722'; Burch & Downe's Garage; several cafés and gas stations; few cabins.) Town is a few hundred yards (L) off US 66. Junction here with US 24. Pike Hotel in Chenoa."

The book was necessarily utilitarian, but not all entries were brief or stiff. At times, nostalgic sentiments seeped through, as in this entry for Texola, Oklahoma:

"159 mi. (114 mi.) TEXOLA. (Pop. 337; alt. 2148'; gas; cafés; no courts; limited facilities.) This sunbaked small town has an old section of stores which truly savor of pioneer days. Notice them to your right on the town's one main cross street. They have sidewalk awnings of wood and metal, supported by posts. Old timers still lounge on the corners."

Rittenhouse, born in Michigan in 1903, had kicked around the publishing business for years, working in sales and advertising and writing for a newspaper. Living in Los Angeles at the end of the war, he was convinced that US 66 would become swamped with tourists. He printed three thousand copies of his guidebook, priced at $1 each, and while his predictions were accurate, a second printing of his book never materialized. Rittenhouse closed out his career in Albuquerque, where he retired from the University of New Mexico Press. In 1988, as the Route 66 renaissance incubated, his former employer honored him by publishing a facsimile of his book. Rittenhouse passed away in 1991. *A Guidebook to Highway 66* is still in print.

* * *

The US Highway 66 Association had been dormant during the war, but was now on a fast track to promoting America's Main Street. In Clinton, Oklahoma, barber Jack Cutberth and his wife, Gladys, attended a local association meeting where Jack agreed to sign on as secretary of the Oklahoma chapter. The Cutberths soon found themselves on the road distributing literature, recruiting members, and making new friends, often for weeks at a time. Their enthusiasm was such that it became a way of life.

In 1954, Jack accepted an offer to become executive secretary of the national organization. During the 16 years he held that position, he became known as "Mr. Route 66," a title he carried with pride for the rest of his life. Gladys once remarked with a nostalgic smile that they made so many trips they wore out a car every year.

This association brochure was widely distributed during the vacation boom years. *Authors' Collection*

Gladys and Jack Cutberth of the US Highway 66 Association. *Courtesy of the late Gladys Cutberth*

In her declining years, she often spoke fondly of their time traveling the route—rewarding years that were well lived and contributed immensely to the welfare of the highway.

* * *

Cars got faster and traffic heavier. Overtaking the sedan in front often included a string of cars holding up the sedan. Such a gamble could cause mom to brace herself with one arm against the dash and the other stretched across the seatback like a railroad barrier for the kids, all the while uttering pleas for deliverance. Getting lost was as easy as a missed turn, and untangling such mistakes could cause nerves to sizzle and play havoc with progress. There were no cell phones, satellite imagery, or navigation systems to assist drivers, nor were there any gaming devices or streaming services to occupy offspring in the back seat. Road trips often included searing heat, flat tires, and a host of other inconveniences. Stopping took place mostly when Dad said so, and if bottles of icy pop were pulled from a machine, odds were good that they were consumed on-site to avoid the penalty of a two-cent deposit. The tradition of "waste not, want not" was a rule to live by. Nothing was disposable.

Yet all of this was background noise compared to the places visited and experiences shared, with the best moments captured on film.

In their backseat domain, Johnny and Suzie entertained themselves discovering

Tourists at Arizona's Canyon Padre Trading Post (later Twin Arrows). *66postcards.com*

Continental Divide was a hot spot for snapshots on the New Mexico route. *Authors' Collection*

animals in the clouds, coloring, reading comic books, or playing license plate games. Boredom inspired either roughhousing or naps, the first likely to activate the long arm of the law up front and the second bringing sighs of relief from the driver and navigator. Motel choices were plentiful. A place where the kids could swim helped wear them out. A diner next door or nearby was all the better.

A sit-down meal brought a satisfying end to the day. Café food was fresh and hot. Coffee steamed, sweet tea crackled with ice, and refills kept coming. Gum-chawing waitresses hustled with endless energy and could recite daily specials like poetry, smiling all the while. Tender pot roast, savory beef stew, pork chops, T-bone steak, and crispy chicken were typical fare. Paired with real mashed potatoes drowned in gravy, fresh vegetables, and hot

Pat Hill Turnbow (L) poses with a friend at her father's Hilltop Trading Post west of Albuquerque, circa 1954. *Courtesy of Vickie Ashcraft*

The U-Drop Inn in Shamrock, Texas, was always ready to satisfy hungry travelers, circa 1940s. *City of Shamrock*

rolls, such feasts foretold a good night's sleep. Pies and cobblers baked that morning filled strategically placed display cases. With the family fed, Mom could replenish the picnic basket at the local grocer for the next day's travel.

Billboards choked the right of way. They advertised amusement parks, outlaw hideouts, trading posts, reptile farms, museums, and every other type of attraction. Scenic wonders, both architectural and natural, took up the slack. When the sun set on cities, the hypnotic glow of electrified glass ruled Main Street. Neon signs flashed, wiggled, pointed, waved, danced, and teased in a kaleidoscope of color. Some spelled out words one letter at a time or featured marquis bulbs that flashed or chased themselves around and around. Catchy names on motels helped seal the deal with the undecided. In Tucumcari alone, the Buckaroo, the Apache, and the Whoa! Palomino were strong draws. Springfield, Illinois, was home to the A. Lincoln Motel. The Wal-A-Pai Court sign in Kingman, Arizona, featured an Indian chief with headdress. Lebanon, Missouri, offered the dreamy Nelson's Dream Village and the mysteriously named Munger Moss Motel. Choosing one over another often came down to strength of the eye candy or whether a pool was part of the package.

The Indian Princess on Oklahoma City's Lincoln Boulevard, in the early 1960s. By then, having a pool was a motel essential. *Authors' Collection*

Kingman, Arizona's Wal-a-Pai Court in the 1950s. *Mohave Museum of History & Arts*

The once inviting Whoa! Palomino motel sign in Tucumcari, New Mexico, is now gone. *John Margolies, Library of Congress*

The 1959 Cadillac Coupe de Ville was king of the tailfin era.
Franksclassiccars.com

Space-age designs, from autos to architecture to kids' toys, were wildly popular by 1959.
From a Kuba Komet catalog

The journey thus became as valued as the destination, with lifetime memories made at roadside attractions and overnight stops. A hot supper and the comfort of an air-conditioned room were worth the price of slowdowns and other annoyances during a day's drive. By the mid-1950s, the "atomic age" dictated trends, and Americans embraced them with gusto. Always looking forward, wage-earners worked hard to elevate their lifestyle and still pinch enough pennies for a summer road trip.

Status symbols were in. Families were judged by the dimensions of their house and model year of their car. Auto makers advanced the space-age vibe with tailfins, and size mattered. On some models they were artfully subtle, on others not so much. The 1959 Cadillac was incomparable for its stylish audacity, with its land-yacht-sized Coupe DeVille weighing in at two-and-a-half tons and sailing down the road at 10 miles per gallon.

Backyard cookouts often involved neighbors and highballs, and most adults smoked. Kids rode bikes with their friends, impersonated cowboys and Indians, watched TV, built forts, and played jacks, hopscotch, and marbles. Gravel lots toughened bare feet at the drive-in theater, where dancing hotdogs on the screen encouraged trips to the concession stand. Pogo sticks and Hula-Hoops were the rage, and teenage girls now swooned to Elvis instead of Sinatra in a sudden coup that left crooners wondering what happened. Dinnertime was a family affair.

* * *

The mid-century vacation boom was vigorously urged along by the US Highway 66 Association. They had dropped the promotional tag "Will Rogers Highway," initially used after Rogers's death in 1935, but renewed it in 1952 when they joined

Drive-ins provided inexpensive family entertainment from the 1940s through the 1970s.
Authors' Collection

Warner Bros. Pictures in promoting *The Will Rogers Story*. For its part, the association organized a caravan that traveled the route from St. Louis to Santa Monica, stopping to install bronze markers in Rogers's honor at each state line. They also made appearances at theaters and various other media events along the way. The publicity generated attracted moviegoers and helped refresh the allure of US 66 in the public eye, similar to what the 1928 Bunion Derby had done.

Even before World War II, US 66 was publicized beyond the efforts of the association. Steinbeck's *The Grapes of Wrath* was released as a motion picture in 1940, prominently featuring the route in film for the first time. Twenty years later, producers Herbert Leonard and Stirling Silliphant created the weekly hit television show *Route 66* for CBS, which ran from 1960 to 1964. Storylines centered on pals Tod Stiles and Buz Murdock bumming around the country in a Corvette, working temporary jobs to fund their exploits. The lead characters, played by Martin Milner and George Maharis, were smart, handsome, honest, and gentlemanly with the ladies. While few episodes were actually filmed on the route, it was the right fit for the times and was unique as the first television series to be shot entirely on location.

Optimism remained high entering the 1960s. Keeping up with the Joneses was at

Boy demonstrates his skill with a Hula-Hoop, first introduced in 1958.
Shorpy, contributed by Islander800

full throttle, and women joined the workforce in growing numbers. Middle-class driveways made room for a second car, and rock 'n' roll was here to stay, despite pushback from older generations. College enrollment was up, and on May 5, 1961, the first suborbital flight took place when Alan Shepard was rocketed into space. Segregation and other unresolved social ills remained, but for many it was a great time to be alive in the USA. Completely unforeseen was the coming upheaval lurking like a drunk driver in a school zone.

* * *

The virtuous tone set for the new decade by TV's Tod and Buz served as a last hurrah for sustaining wholesome values, which were soon derailed by acute shifts in culture and politics. The 1962 Cuban missile crisis sobered the nation and brought the Cold War into grim perspective. This, followed by President Kennedy's 1963 assassination, cast a pall over the pursuit of happiness. As the Boomer generation came of age, they began to express themselves in ways that went beyond changes in dress, jargon, and rebellious

The US Highway 66 Association capitalized on the popularity of the TV show. *Authors' Collection*

The Will Rogers Caravan makes a scheduled stop at the Kirkwood (Missouri) Theater in 1952. *66postcards.com*

behavior seen in the past. Within a year of *Route 66's* final episode, the definition of heroes and villains had blurred, and as the Vietnam War escalated, so did youthful assertiveness. Protestors filled the streets, demanding answers and spreading the mantra "don't trust anyone over 30." Broadcast television kept them informed and ensured their message was heard.

Social mores of the 1950s underwent serious reconstruction, but they did not disappear entirely. The motion picture industry, for example, was slow to let go of traditional themes. It was 1969 before films like *Easy Rider* and *Midnight Cowboy* replaced escapism with reality. Television continued to serve up variety shows, westerns, and sitcoms, partly in denial and partly to offer shelter from the daily news. Protest songs consumed only a small share of radio airtime. It was an unsettling mix. 1969 was the year of the first moon landing, a monumental achievement. It was also the year of Woodstock, the Manson murders, and the Chappaquiddick scandal. Bob Dylan warned in 1964 that the times were changing, but few were prepared for turbulence seismic enough to redirect the future.

Nearly two million young Americans were inducted into the armed forces, while others defiantly burned their draft cards. Some "dropped out," becoming hippies with no plan and no solutions. A relatively small number became radicalized. By the mid-1960s there were "sit-ins," marches, and campus uprisings. Clashes between "peaceniks" and "hardhats" deepened the divide, and militant groups such as the Weather Underground sought change through violence. The drug culture exploded and wrecked thousands of lives. At the same time, the civil rights movement tore at the seams of the nation.

It was a decade of cultural schizophrenia and a widening generation gap. Adults still went to work, paid bills, and kept one eye on their career ladders. Their kids wrestled with the angst of reconciling allegiance to wayward peers with the traditions of their upbringing. They were, after all, the sons and daughters of World War II veterans. Changing realities left them conflicted, but despite the turmoil, most were no less dedicated to chasing the opposite sex, lusting after muscle cars, or fixating on the British music invasion.

Through it all, society's windows rattled, but never broke. And while there were casualties all around, most Americans maintained their footing and weathered the storm.

Route 66 had no such luck.

The 1960s found US 66 ascending the steps of the gallows. Its popularity had made it a victim of its own success, a self-strangulating and unavoidable eventuality. The physical roadbed had been battered by military convoys during the war, and the ensuing vacation boom brought unbearable levels of traffic. Repairs and upgrades couldn't keep up. The answer, predetermined in the 1950s, was to revolutionize the motoring landscape with a new system of interstate highways. It would be a long and painful process executed with relentless force.

Muscle cars like this 1966 Chevy Chevelle SS 396 dominated the youth car market. *Courtesy of Admcars.com*

A hippie at a demonstration shares his preferences for life's priorities. *Creative Commons*

Live appearances by the Beatles almost always triggered fan hysteria, 1964. *Marion S Trikosko, Library of Congress*

Neon

NEON TUGS at the eye like gravity. In its presence, to look elsewhere is difficult. It combines bold colors with mesmerizing iridescence. In form it is limitless. Its glass tubes can be bent and twisted into any shape, restrained only by the skill of the bender. Blueprints can be as basic as a single stick of glass or as complex as animated galloping horses. When the switch is flipped, dazzling light consumes its surroundings and captivates beholders.

The emergence of electrified gas coincided nicely with the evolution of the route. Neon was discovered in London in 1898 by chemists Sir William Ramsay and Morris Travers after removing oxygen, nitrogen, and argon from air, which caused it to glow bright red when electrically charged. Professor Ramsay, who had already discovered argon and helium, was knighted in 1902 and awarded the Nobel Prize in 1904. Neon's application to advertising followed, with the first commercial use of an outdoor sign in the United States credited to Packard dealer Earle Anthony of Los Angeles in 1923.

A truck from Star Neon Sign Company is loaded for delivery and installation. *Authors' Collection*

Sir William Ramsay, the father of neon (1852–1916). *Nobel Foundation Archive via Wikipedia Commons*

By the end of the 1930s, neon signs could be found showcasing motels, gas stations, beer joints, cafés, hardware stores, theaters, drug stores, barber shops, car lots, and just about every other business that wanted business. Along US 66, waves of throbbing color drenched city Main Streets end to end, festively illuminating the lonesome darkness.

These works of roadside art have entranced shutterbugs since the days of the Brownie. Whether creating simple memories or documenting roadside vernacular, neon signs are a subject anyone with a camera feels compelled to photograph. While changing trends and the expense of maintenance caused the number of signs to thin dramatically by the 1970s, the route's renaissance brought renewed demand, and neon shops are now as busy as they once were.

Neon began to wane by the 1970s, as seen in this Shamrock, Texas, street view.
Courtesy of Jerry McClanahan

Buck Atoms Curios in Tulsa has raised the bar for new Route 66 attractions with this "cosmic" display.
Courtesy of Mary Beth Babcock

Oklahoma City's Boyer Hotel Court sign included arrow-shooting animation.
Photo by Donald M. Fuller, Elizabeth Hay Collection, Courtesy Oklahoma Historical Society

Multiple colors and bulbs help distinguish the Western Hills Motel in Flagstaff, Arizona.
Courtesy of Jim Ross

The Luna Café in Mitchell, Illinois, a former speakeasy, has been in business since 1924.
Courtesy of Jim Thole

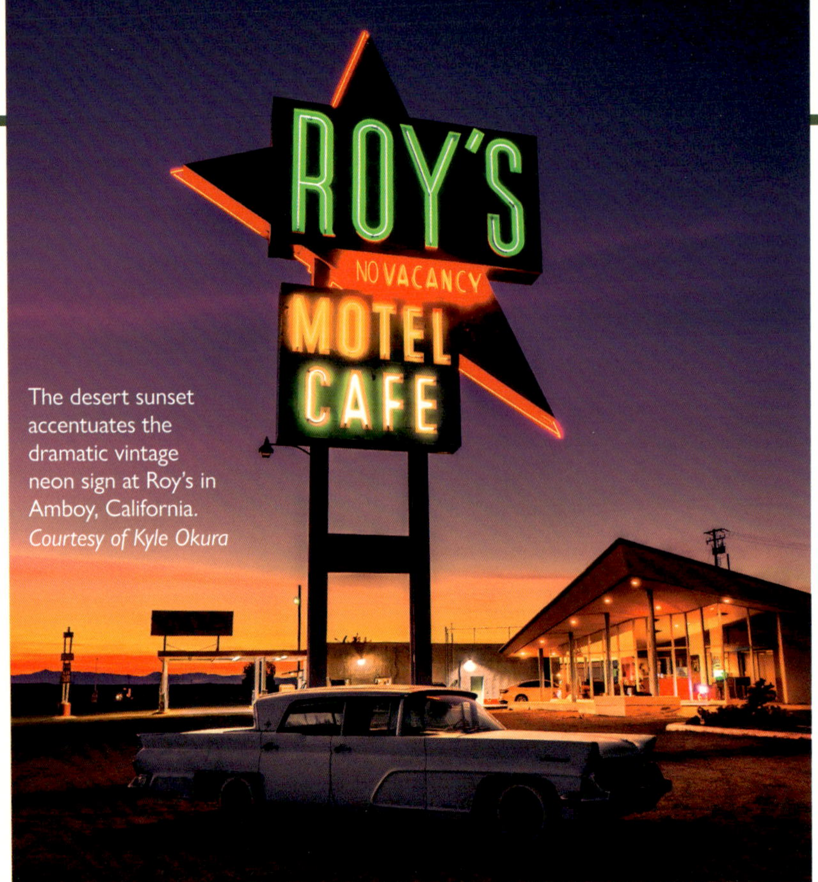

The desert sunset accentuates the dramatic vintage neon sign at Roy's in Amboy, California.
Courtesy of Kyle Okura

Neon as art can be striking, as seen in this Alison LaMons watercolor on paper.
Courtesy of Alison LaMons, www.alisonstudios.com

Gallup, New Mexico's Chamber of Commerce presents a strong visual of the Route 66 experience with this neon display.
Original art for sign and photo by Jerry McClanahan

The Gardenway Motel in Gray Summit, Missouri, was lost to the wrecking ball in 2023. *Courtesy of Shellee Graham*

Detail shot of the Charcoal Oven, an Oklahoma City institution now gone. *Courtesy of Jim Ross*

The intricate and stunning El Don Motel sign in Albuquerque. *Courtesy of Shellee Graham*

Tucumcari's Blue Swallow Motel features a downsized replica of its original sign. *Courtesy of Kevin Mueller*

Five Harvey Girls strike a pose in this vintage portrait circa 1910. *Kolb, Emery, Northern Arizona University, Cline Library*

CHAPTER 7

Ladies of Legend

THROUGH THE AGES, women have demonstrated their tenacity, and with the coming of the auto age the need to broaden their horizons found new outlets. In what was then considered a man's world, women broke that barrier to chart their own course. They completed cross-country road trips, rode motorcycles, piloted airplanes, learned trades dominated by men, and otherwise refused to accept as limitations the traditional roles imposed upon them. Once free of those bonds, opportunities for achievement stretched before them like an endless ribbon of road. Route 66 attracted its share of these resolute ladies, and the story of the highway would be incomplete without recognizing them.

A woman strikes a pose with an early 20th century Indian motorcycle. *Authors' Collection*

Blue Swallow owner Lillian Redman in her motel office, 1990s. *Courtesy of Hiroshi Hanamura*

The Blue Swallow with its original sign, circa 1950s. *Authors' Collection*

* * *

The highway of dreams for Lillian Beatrice Leigon was US 66. Born in Granbury, Texas, to Sallie and Grover Leigon in 1909, Lillian traveled with her parents and three siblings in 1915 from Clifton, Texas, to eastern New Mexico in a covered wagon. It took four months. There the family homesteaded in a dugout on the Llano Estacado's caprock southeast of Tucumcari. For Lillian, it was an upbringing no less challenging than that of the pioneers. In 1923, as she entered her teens, the family moved to Tucumcari, where her father worked for the railroad. Following graduation, Lillian attended business school in Kansas, then returned to Tucumcari to work as a secretary.

Lillian soon took to the road, her urge to roam stoked by her childhood. She cooked and waitressed in Arizona, where she found work with the Fred Harvey Company at Grand Canyon's El Tovar. While there she married Glenn Roper, but that union ended in 1956, and Lillian went back to Tucumcari, where in 1958 she became involved with the recently divorced Floyd Redman. Floyd was a man of means, and Lillian worked for him as a bookkeeper and waitress until they married in 1964.

To celebrate, Floyd bought the Blue Swallow Court for his bride, knowing that Lillian's background made her well suited to run a motel. The motor court was built in 1939 by local carpenter W. A. Huggins, initially with 10 units. In 1944 it was acquired by Ted and Marjorie Jones. Ted Jones died in 1952, and the motel was sold. By 1960, two rooms had been added and the manager's residence enlarged by absentee owner Dan Holmes, from whom Floyd Redman acquired the property. The only significant change thereafter was the addition of a large, drive-under sign.

For 34 years, Lillian's devotion to

the Blue Swallow was unshakable. She relished bringing the world to her doorstep and bestowed her guests with comfort and warmth. A copy of a benediction she crafted was left in each room, which read, in part: "We are all travelers. From 'birth till death,' we travel between the eternities. May these days be pleasant for you, profitable for society, helpful for those you meet, and a joy to those you know and love best. Sincerely yours, Lillian Redman."

Over the years, Lillian and the Blue Swallow were featured in *Life*, *Arizona Highways*, and *National Geographic*, among other publications. Floyd passed away in 1973, and eight years later Tucumcari was bypassed by I-40. Lillian was 71 then, alone, and her only source of income was threatened, but she refused to quit. It wasn't until 1998 that she finally relinquished her beloved motel. Even then, she made frequent visits there until she peacefully passed away the following year at age 89, having lived a life that assured her a lasting place in the lore of the highway.

* * *

Photographer Dorothea Lange spent the 1930s roaming Route 66 and other states in the South and West to capture on film the

Dorothea Lange on the road in 1936.
Photo by Lange assistant Rondal Partridge, Library of Congress

A typical migrant camp shanty near Weedpatch, California, 1940. *Dorothea Lange, Library of Congress*

struggles of Depression-era Americans. The result was an archive of images that profoundly portrays the despair and hopelessness of displaced families during one of our nation's darkest periods.

Lange's own struggles included a childhood marred by illness and disruption. Born May 26, 1895, to German immigrant parents as Dorothea Margaretta Nutzhorn in Hoboken, New Jersey, she contracted polio at age 7, which disfigured her right leg. Five years later she endured the pain of abandonment when her father deserted the family. These experiences figured prominently in shaping her adult life, as she developed a sensitivity to others burdened with undeserved hardships.

After high school, Lange worked as a portrait photographer and attended Columbia University's Teachers College, where she studied under renowned photographer Clarence H. White. Following a year of international travel in 1918, Dorothea opened a portrait studio in San Francisco, where she began using her mother's maiden name of Lange as her own. There she met artist Maynard Dixon. They married in 1920 and by 1928 were the parents of two sons. Life was good, if predictable, until the stock market crash permanently altered Dorothea's future. As job seekers filled the streets, studio portraiture landed on life support, and this prompted her to turn her lens outward. In only a short time, her poignant images of destitute Americans began to receive notice.

Agricultural economist and professor Paul Taylor had seen one of Lange's exhibitions, and at his invitation she made her first trip to a migrant camp during the 1934 pea harvest in Nipomo, California. Lange and Taylor quickly became more than colleagues and were married in 1935 following Lange's divorce from Dixon. They had a working relationship throughout their marriage and often traveled together. What Dorothea witnessed during her encounters with migrants set the trajectory of her career—influencing social change through photography. She went to work for the Resettlement Administration and began documenting homeless and migrant families along Route 66 and elsewhere. Wherever they drifted to, or from, she was there, capturing their expressions of uncertainty, bewilderment, and loss.

A collection of her work, *An American Exodus: A Record of Human Erosion*, was published in 1939, and in 1941 she received a Guggenheim fellowship. Dorothea's legacy was secured, but she wasn't finished. Her lens next focused on the World War II incarceration of Japanese Americans, which she vehemently opposed. She accepted a job with the War Relocation Authority to document their internment, but the images she submitted conveyed criticism of the policy and were suppressed by the government. More than 60 years later, in 2006, that work was published under the title *Impounded: Dorothea Lange and the Censored Images of Japanese American Internment*. By then, she was already a member of the National Women's Hall of Fame, having been inducted in 2003.

In the post-war era, Lange concentrated on photo essays and curating exhibitions for New York's Museum of Modern Art. Paul Taylor resumed his teaching duties full-time at UC Berkeley. He passed away at age 89, outliving his wife by 19 years. Dorothea had fought chronic health issues since the 1940s, due in part to post-polio syndrome, but it was esophageal cancer that claimed her life on October 11, 1965. At the time, she was living in San Francisco, ending her epic journey where it began.

Migrants stopped along the roadside in Lordsburg, New Mexico, talking things over. *Dorothea Lange, Library of Congress*

Winslow, Arizona's Harvey House lunchroom in the Santa Fe Station and Hotel circa 1920, prior to construction of La Posada. *Arizona Memory Project, Arizona State Library*

* * *

The shiny rails of the Atchison, Topeka, and Santa Fe Railroad stretched across the sparsely populated West like a path to nowhere, and this presented a workforce challenge for hotelier Fred Harvey (1835–1901). Harvey's partnership with the railroad, which began in the 1870s, led to a string of luxury hotels designed and built for the railroad by Harvey's company over the next 40 years. At its peak, the Fred Harvey Company managed more than 80 dining room and hotel locations. Harvey House hotels along what became Route 66 included La Fonda in Santa Fe, the Alvarado in Albuquerque, La Posada in Winslow, the Fray Marcos in Williams, Escalante in Ash Fork, the Havasu in Seligman, El Garces in Needles, and El Desierto in Barstow. El Tovar and Bright Angel Lodge, north of the route at the Grand Canyon, were reached by train from Williams.

Staffing the hotels and dining rooms required a renewable source of ladies, a problem Harvey solved by recruiting in the East, offering unattached prospects a chance to become independent and find adventure in the untamed West. It was a message that resonated with women seeking just that. They were given one-year employment contracts that included room and board and the opportunity to escape dead-end lives. In exchange, they were required to abide by strict rules. "Harvey Girls" had to be of good character and exhibit impeccable manners. They wore a uniform consisting of a long black dress, white apron, and black hosiery with black shoes. Linens had to be spotless, place settings exact. Coffee urns were refreshed every two hours. They lived under curfew in dormitories supervised by the most senior staffer among them. In the early years, getting married meant leaving the company, though for those hoping to find a husband, and many did, working for Fred Harvey provided a prime opportunity.

The following poem, by Leiger Mitchell Hodges, added polish to their social standing. It appeared in the *Philadelphia North American* on May 5, 1905.

I have seen some splendid paintings in my day,
And I have looked at faultless statuary;
I have seen the orchard trees a-bloom in May,
And watched their colors in the shadows vary;
I have viewed the noblest shrines in Italy,
And gazed upon the richest mosques of Turkey—
But the fairest of all sights, it seems to me,
Was the Harvey Girl I saw in Albuquerque.

Harvey died in 1901, but his business empire grew under the leadership of his son Ford Harvey, and as the 20th century stretched its legs, restrictions relaxed. Harvey Girls could marry and keep their jobs, and age requirements quietly went away.

Harvey Girl Jeannie Elizabeth Williamson in Seligman, Arizona, 1930.
History and Archives Division, Arizona State Library, Archives and Public Records

By the 1930s, thousands of girls had become part of the unique sorority that earned them the title "Harvey Girl." One of them was Jeannie Elizabeth Williamson, born the youngest of seven children in 1902 in Miller, Missouri, west of Springfield and only two miles north of the future Route 66 village of Albatross. She was just 16 when she lost her mother at age 57 to illness and only 20 when her brother died in 1922 from a job-related fall at age 31. She was still with the family then in Kansas City, Kansas, but would make the leap to Seligman, Arizona, the same year, where she and her sister Rowena became Harvey Girls. Jeannie was 28 when her photo was taken in 1930 at Seligman's Havasu Harvey House.

Jeannie married Chester Sharar, an accountant, in 1923, and they lived in Seligman until moving to Winslow in the early 1930s. By then she had given birth to three daughters. A fourth daughter was tragically lost shortly after delivery. Her husband, Chester, active in water sports and golf, died in 1959 from a heart attack while boating. He was 62. Jeannie lived for another 32 years and

Dorothy Hunt as a Harvey Girl at Bright Angel Lodge at the Grand Canyon, 1946. *History and Archives Division, Arizona State Library, Archives and Public Records*

never remarried. She was living in Show Low, Arizona, when she joined her husband in 1991 at age 89. They are buried together in Winslow's Desert View Cemetery.

Dorothy Hunt, at age 29, was already married when she joined the staff at Grand Canyon's Bright Angel Lodge in 1945. Born Dorothy Bailey in St. Johns, Arizona, in 1916, she was only 2 when she lost an infant sister, Lena, and at age 11 suffered the loss of her two-year-old brother Robert. Her family lived in Hemet, California, during her teen years, but by 1940 had returned to Arizona, settling in Winslow. Dorothy found work as a waitress, married Richard Hunt in 1944, and became a Harvey Girl the next year. She and her husband had two children, Richard and Leslie.

By 1950 Dorothy had left Bright Angel Lodge to manage Hunt's Feed and Supply and the Wranglers 4-H Club with her husband in Winslow. Not one to sit on her hands, she studied genealogy and worked occasional shifts at Fred Harvey's La Posada. She also traveled extensively, selling and trading Indian jewelry across the Southwest. Dorothy Bailey Hunt lived to be 89, surviving her husband Richard by 11 years. She is now at rest in St. Johns, Arizona, the place of her birth.

Life for the average Harvey Girl may have been unremarkable, but as a group they stood apart. Most were driven toward self-betterment by foregoing the security of familiar surroundings to independently try something daring and new during an era when the majority of women were expected to live uneventful lives. They helped civilize the western frontier when outlaws still roamed the land and otherwise distinguished themselves in ways that enriched both the folklore of the Southwest and the history of the route.

* * *

Motoring the Mother Road was not limited to the Caucasian majority, whether traveling for pleasure or business, and for minorities it meant coping with resistance and, at times, outright hostility. Planning a successful trip included the need to know where the restaurants, gas stations, and hotels were that accepted them. This need was first filled in 1936 with the publication of *The Negro Travelers' Green Book*, which was updated annually. One listing in the 1950s for Springfield, Missouri, was for Alberta's Hotel.

Alberta's Farm provided a place of refuge and relaxation. *Missouri State University Libraries, Special Collections and Archives, Logan Collection*

Alberta Ellis with grandson Irv Logan, circa 1946.
Missouri State University Libraries, Special Collections and Archives, Logan Collection

Alberta's Hotel at 617 South Benton Avenue in Springfield, Missouri.
Missouri State University Libraries, Special Collections and Archives, Logan Collection

Alberta Ellis was a well-dressed woman who carried herself with an air of self-assurance. Born Margie Alberta Northcutt on December 27, 1909, to Clarence Northcutt and Ora Crittenden of Springfield, she would prove to have a head for business and be driven by a sense of civic duty. In 1926 she married Fred Watkins in Kansas City and in 1927 gave birth to a daughter, Ora Elizabeth. Alberta worked primarily as a housekeeper until 1947, when better pay and job security came her way with a position at Southwestern Bell Telephone. Her story could have ended there, but in 1952 an opportunity for her to make a difference presented itself.

Springfield's City Hospital, where people of color could receive care, had closed. The three-story residential structure was located on Benton Avenue one block south of City US 66. Now divorced and again using her maiden name, Alberta bought the building with help from family members for $10,000 and converted it into a hotel, adding a snack bar, dining room, barber shop, and beauty salon, all the while working her regular job. By the late 1950s she had married Robert Ellis of nearby Lebanon and became stepmother to his young daughter, Paula.

When word of Alberta's hotel got around, it became *the* place in Springfield for African American travelers, including celebrity guests Nat King Cole, the Harlem Globetrotters, and singer Frankie Lyman. Alberta broadened her domain with the acquisition of the Crystal Lounge, a club located on the route in west Springfield. She also bought a house and acreage a few miles

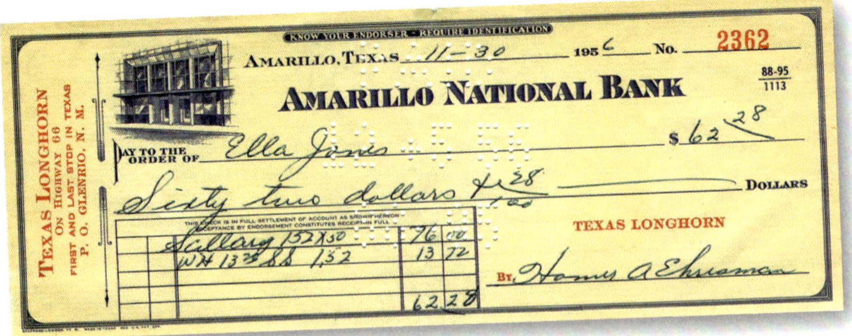

KNOW YOUR ENDORSER - REQUIRE IDENTIFICATION

TEXAS LONGHORN
ON HIGHWAY 66
FIRST AND LAST STOP IN TEXAS
P. O. GLENRIO, N. M.

AMARILLO, TEXAS 11-30 1956 No. 2362

AMARILLO NATIONAL BANK

88-95
1113

PAY TO THE ORDER OF Ella Jones $62.28

Sixty two dollars & 28/100 DOLLARS

TEXAS LONGHORN

A canceled payroll check from the Texas Longhorn made out to Ella Jones. *Authors' Collection*

Glenrio's Texas Longhorn Café enjoyed brisk business in the 1950s. *Authors' Collection*

farther out dubbed "The Farm," which was used as a weekend getaway and as a safe place for travelers and friends to relax, picnic, and socialize.

By the end of the 1950s, Alberta recognized that progress with integration would soon diminish the need for her hotel. The Civil Rights Act of 1964 facilitated this coming change, but before Alberta could determine the hotel's future, the city acquired it through eminent domain, which they had pursued throughout her ownership. This was not unexpected. What she could not foresee was that her health would soon fail. Alberta Northcutt Ellis was stricken with liver cancer and in 1966 passed away at the youthful age of 56, ending any plans she may have had to further serve her community. Now resting in Springfield's Lincoln Memorial Park Cemetery, she is remembered by travelers and civil rights advocates alike for her invaluable contributions during difficult times.

* * *

Throughout the route's lifespan, the majority of those employed by roadside enterprises never distinguished themselves beyond showing up for work. Thousands of unsung cashiers, station attendants, hash slingers, mechanics, maids, clerks, waitresses, and other worker bees quietly slipped unnoticed into the fog of history, reduced to names on headstones and faded photos in dusty attics. It was only through a café owner's failure to destroy business records that a link to one of them serendipitously surfaced. Her name was Ella Jones.

The life of Glenrio, Texas, which straddles the state line with New Mexico, essentially ended in 1973 when I-40 cleaved US 66 at both ends of town. Left in the interstate's wake was a single point of access, ominously numbered Exit 0. Today, only battered ruins remain. Broken windows rattle and corroded hinges creak when the wind howls, and cranky dogs yap at curious tires rolling over grainy asphalt. A few steadfast residents cling to homesteads here; everything else is decomposing, inching its way into the earth. Inside the remains of a moldy motel room and nestled deep within a heap of water-stained bank statements, a canceled payroll check from the Texas Longhorn was randomly pulled from an envelope in 1997. It was dated November 30, 1956, and made out to Ella Jones. The amount was for $62.28, which represented take-home pay for 152 hours worked that month at 50 cents per hour.

She was born Mattie Ella Whitten in 1909 to Euclid and Ada

Whitten at Arch, New Mexico. In August 1925 she left her parents and two brothers to marry ranch hand Tom Jones in Glenrio. She was 16. Only a month later, her father Euclid was killed in a fall from a horse while driving cattle. At 17 Ella gave birth to a daughter, Ruth, in Adrian, Texas, and in 1936 delivered a son, Charles, who was born in Amarillo. Husband Tom sought employment where it could be found. They lived and worked variously in Adrian, Texas, as well as Glenrio and Endee, New Mexico, and surrounding areas.

Homer and Margaret Ehresman built the Texas Longhorn station and café in 1953, adding a motel in 1955. Under the banner "We Never Close," they enjoyed brisk business, serving truckers, travelers, and locals alike. Cooks and waitresses worked tiring hours for low pay and skimpy tips, serving up coffee and pie and steamy plate dinners to an endless parade of growling stomachs. With few nonagricultural jobs available between Adrian, Texas, to the east and Tucumcari, New Mexico, to the west, Ella's employment at the Longhorn was likely an extended affair, though perhaps intermittent. Tom worked as a laborer, ranch hand, and station attendant wherever he could hire on, but he always called Glenrio home.

The Texas Longhorn Café in a state of ruin, 2016.
Courtesy of Shellee Graham

It is not known whether Ella was a housekeeper at the motel or worked in the café, or both, but she was rarely more than a short drive away during her adult life. Tom died in their Glenrio home in 1964 at age 62. Ella joined him at age 60 after a short stay in an Amarillo hospital in 1969. They, along with son Charles, who died in 1994, are buried in Memorial Park Cemetery in Vega, Texas. The Texas Longhorn closed in 1976, three years after Glenrio was bypassed.

Ella was born a farm girl who braved the lean years of the Great Depression and Dust Bowl. Life never got much easier, and she died young, predeceasing her mother Ada by 10 years. But she embodied the spirit of the times, when folks earned their way without complaint and were thankful for what they had. The ratio of happiness to sorrow that shaped Ella's faith and worldview may never be known, but her story reminds us that those who work mundane jobs and seldom see a nod of approval are the true lifeblood of the route.

* * *

Joyce Withington Nevin began life in 1924 as the daughter of Rhode Islanders Margaret and Benjamin Nevin. Joy, as she chose to be called, graduated from the Mary C. Wheeler School of Providence in 1942. A talented and active student, she also helped out at the family farm in nearby Rice City. While attending the School of Horticulture in Ambler, Pennsylvania, in 1943, Joy became engaged to Ensign Elton Wayne Cooke of Patchogue, Long Island, New York, a Brown University graduate and a pilot with the Naval Air Corps, stationed in Alaska.

In a letter to her fiancé's parents, Lillian and Harry Cooke, dated February 12, 1943, Joy wrote:

"I feel the war will be over soon and he'll be back before we know it. It certainly was hard for us to say goodbye." On March

Joy Nevin in a 1941 high school talent contest. *Courtesy of David Coward, curator of the Coward-Cooke Family Website*

6, she included this sentiment in another letter to her future in-laws: "I've been awful busy with school & writing to Cookie. We are both terribly lonesome for each other."

Joy left school at semester's end to work the family farm after her father became ill, but "Cookie" was foremost on her mind. On May 14, 1943, a telegram from the War Department informed Elton's parents that their son had gone missing during a patrol of the Aleutian Islands. With the war raging, the search for his PV-1 Ventura bomber soon ended. Joy, though in despair from the news, expressed confidence that he would return.

She took action by joining the Women Airforce Service Pilots (WASP), which trained women to fly non-combat missions. She completed the year-long program, but it was disbanded before she was activated due to political pressure triggered by pilot deaths. She considered joining the navy's WAVES, but instead enrolled in Rhode Island's Bryant College to study business. In March 1945 she wrote to Elton's parents: "I watch the papers each night, hoping that I'll see that maybe Cookie is in one of these prison camps. I have never once felt that he wasn't coming home." The war ended in August 1945 as Joy finished college, and the nation began the long process of putting the heartaches it had imposed behind them. Elton Wayne Cooke was never heard from again.

Joy had inherited the farm, and in September she was featured in *The Rhode Islander* magazine for succeeding where few women had. Then, in 1946, she was hospitalized with polio. In early 1948, mostly recovered, she sold everything and hit the road, ending up in Heber, Arizona, where a friend and her husband owned the Gibson Ranch. Joy walked with a limp, but she could ride, and the Gibsons offered her work. Having gained a foothold, Joy bought a panel truck, which doubled as

Joy with Elton Wayne "Cookie" Cooke before his deployment to Alaska. *Courtesy of David Coward, curator of the Coward-Cooke Family Website*

Joy Nevin during WASP flight training in 1943. *Courtesy of David Coward, curator of the Coward-Cooke Family Website*

her home, and launched Stockmen's Supply Service, selling area ranchers everything from leather punches and rope to tick killer and ammunition from her store on wheels. Business was good, and in 1950 she was profiled in *Arizona Cattlelog*, a news magazine for the ranching community.

Scouting for customers eventually led her to the Painted Desert Trading Post, whose owner, Dotch Windsor, maintained a small herd of cattle and horses. Though 28 years her senior, the ruggedly handsome Dotch soon struck up a romance with Joy, who by then was ready to end her loneliness but had found ranch hands her own age too unsettled. They married in 1950, and their daughter, Addilade "Dee" Windsor, was born in 1952. Desert life at the trading post was demanding but not without occasional excitement, as Joy's aviation skills came in handy the day a single-engine plane appeared overhead, tipping its wings in distress. She signaled to a store clerk to help stop traffic on the highway, assisted with the landing, and had a nice chat with the pilot while topping off his nearly empty tanks.

Things had changed dramatically by 1954. Joy's marriage was crumbling, and a proposed relocation of US 66 threatened to isolate their business. Her divorce from Dotch became final in 1956, and two years later traffic in front of the trading post evaporated when the new highway opened one mile to the south.

Dotch Windsor closed up and moved to Holbrook, where he died in 1964 at age 68. Joy returned to Rhode Island, married and divorced a second time, and in 1970 returned to Holbrook, where she was briefly married a third time. Having given up ranch life, she became a community leader and citizens' advocate. She kept the weather station and spearheaded efforts to complete Holbrook's Senior Citizens Center and Extended Care Facility, of which she later became director. For this she was honored in Washington, DC, as a recipient of the Louise B. Gerrard Award for outstanding

Dotch and Joy Windsor's Painted Desert Trading Post 60 years after abandonment. *Courtesy of Rob Medlin*

Joy and Dotch Windsor, circa 1953. *Courtesy of Adela Windsor*

service to rural elderly Americans. Joy Nevin passed away in 1998 at age 73. In recognition of her contributions to her adopted hometown, a segment of original US 66 in Holbrook now bears her name.

* * *

These women stand out but do not stand alone. They are joined by a regiment of others whose achievements and influence added luster to the Route 66 star. Their contributions, both collectively and individually, flavored the world around them and added greatly to the rich history of the route. Their stories are the story of the road.

The iconic billboard at Arizona's Jack Rabbit Trading Post.
Cindy Blansett Jaquez Photo, courtesy of the Jack Rabbit Trading Post

CHAPTER 8

Trading Posts and Tourist Traps

HROUGHOUT THE POSTWAR vacation boom, the Route 66 roadside was rife with trading posts, especially in the West. In places, so many occupied the same stretch of highway it was as if they had battled to claim a constricted vein of gold. In eastern Arizona, the Painted Desert Trading Post, Painted Desert Park, Painted Desert Tower, Painted Desert Inn, and Painted Desert Point all occupied the same 10-mile length of roadway. Whether their relative proximity hurt or helped, it gave kids in the back seat five opportunities in 15 minutes to bend Dad's ear about stopping.

Most trading posts of the era could be likened to the merging of a gift shop with a convenience store. Offerings included sundries, fuel, and Native American wares, both genuine and those mass produced as souvenirs. Many had cafés, and some had overnight accommodations.

At Lupton, Arizona, Max and Amelia Ortega opened the Indian Trail Trading Post in 1946 on land gifted to them by the railroad after Max saved the life of a rail worker. Its appeal was hard to resist, especially for westbound travelers, given that the next sizable city, Holbrook, was over 70 miles away. The Indian Trail stayed busy until its future was nullified by the completion of I-40, which left it with its back to the interstate a half mile west of the Lupton exit. Despite this loss, the Ortegas persevered, and the extended family continues to operate numerous roadside businesses in the region.

Max Ortega's Indian Trail Trading Post at Lupton, Arizona. *Steve Rider Collection*

Eight miles west of Lupton, the Yellowhorse Trading Post was opened in the early 1960s by three brothers—Juan, Frank, and Shush Yellowhorse, sons of full-blooded Navajo Anna Yellowhorse. Interstate construction soon forced a relocation to Lupton, where they built a five-story teepee called Fort Yellowhorse. After it was suspiciously lost to fire in 1971, a new store was constructed nearby and has served travelers since, using bold colors and highway billboards to attract customers. The brothers are now gone (Juan became a Navajo chief), but the trading post remains. Its visibility, combined with a spectacular rock bluff looming overhead and easy access from I-40, has helped ensure its longevity.

Lupton, Arizona's Yellowhorse Travel Center continues in business alongside I-40. *Courtesy of Jim Ross*

The Jack Rabbit Trading Post was built by Jim Taylor just west of Joseph City, Arizona, in 1949. Glenn Blansett bought it

The site of Twin Arrows Trading Post, formerly the Canyon Padre Trading Post, 2000. *Courtesy of Jim Ross*

The Navajo Trading Post, an early tenant at Continental Divide, New Mexico. *66postcards.com*

The enduring Jack Rabbit Trading Post in the 1950s. *Courtesy of the Jack Rabbit Trading Post*

in 1967, and it has been in the family since, now in the capable hands of Cindy Blansett Jaquez and her husband, Tony. One of the oldest still in business, its distinctive "Here It Is!" billboard and larger-than-life rabbit have been entertaining families since the beginning. Not as fortunate was Twin Arrows, formerly the Canyon Padre Trading Post near Winona, which survived interstate bypass but was finally abandoned in 1995. The same fate befell Ella's Frontier in Joseph City, which stood vacant for decades before being razed in 2022.

The intersection of Route 66 and the Continental Divide east of Gallup, New Mexico, has been a prime business location since the highway's earliest days, and remains so. Just west of Albuquerque, the Hilltop Trading Post later became today's Enchanted Trails RV Park and Trading Post. Elsewhere in the western states,

Queenan's Trading Post on the west edge of Elk City, Oklahoma.
Courtesy of the late Wanda Queenan

The Longhorn Ranch east of Moriarty, New Mexico, was a premier Wild West attraction.
Authors' Collection

trading posts have generally gone to ruin or disappeared. Of those still operating, most are of the interstate era or located near cities.

Trading post numbers along the route sharply declined east of New Mexico. Oklahoma was home to a handful, including Queenan's in Elk City, Wolf Robe Hunt's in Tulsa, and Buffalo Dill's east of Vinita. All of these are now gone, and only a scant few, such as Rolla, Missouri's Mule Trading Post (now closed), existed eastward from Oklahoma.

* * *

The term "tourist trap" could be considered a slur. The connotation leans negative, though not all of them, such as amusement parks and Wild West attractions, engaged in trickery. More apt to wear

The Hilltop Trading Post atop Nine Mile Hill west of Albuquerque was remodeled regularly by owner L. G. Hill.
Steve Rider Collection

Jake and Maxine Atkinson's Rattle Snake Trading Post at Bluewater, New Mexico. *Authors' Collection*

that label would be reptile farms and animal zoos. Trading posts enjoyed more respectability, though the distinctions between the two grew a bit hazy when some trading posts added "live" attractions and used billboards that overpromised. One notable crossover was Jake and Maxine Atkinson's Rattle Snake Trading Post at Bluewater, New Mexico. Now a roadside ruin, it once offered the best of both worlds.

Because tourist traps sold an "experience," their advertising wasn't bound by the truth. Carnival-style props and deceptive billboards were among the tools used to cause foot pressure on brake pedals, especially for the tackier attractions. A Carlsbad, New Mexico, newspaper in 1953 described the infestation of billboards as "lurid and gaudy." Route 66 motorists in New Mexico and Arizona during that era were confronted by the following signs, among others: "NEXT STOP—MAN KILLING BOA CONSTRICTOR"; "MOST VICIOUS ANIMAL ALIVE—

J. T. Turner's Tomahawk Trading Post west of Albuquerque was a tourist trap crossover, featuring teepees, reptiles, burro rides, and Native American dancers. *66postcards.com*

Regal Reptile Ranch in Alanreed, Texas, the last of the snake farms.
Courtesy of Joel Rayburn

MAN EATING WILDCATS"; and "NEXT STOP—SEE GIANT PREHISTORIC REPTILE—48 FEET LONG!"

Not surprisingly, the more provocative the advertising, the stronger the pull. Like rubberneckers at accidents, it aroused motorists' fear and loathing, even when the encounter left them disturbed or disgruntled rather than thrilled or amazed. One of the most notorious was the Regal Reptile Ranch in Alanreed, Texas, which wasn't the biggest of its breed, but was the longest-lasting.

Few hucksters on the route exploited slithering serpents better than siblings Mike and Addie Allred, whose Regal Reptile Ranch opened first in Elk City, Oklahoma, in the 1950s. In 1970, highway construction forced a move westward to near Texola. Just five years later, when I-40 was extended to the Texas line, they moved again to their final location in Alanreed, Texas. Things went well until brother and sister had a falling out, at which point Mike bagged his vipers and left. He leased a former gas station five miles east of nearby McLean that featured a giant neon steer's head impossible to miss. He christened his new place "Reptiles Galore," and with help from building owner C. R. Cunningham erected a towering sign in a nearby pasture

Tourist trap billboards were a common sight along the New Mexico roadside in the 1950s.
66postcards.com

After a severe storm blew down the "Rattlesnakes – Exit Now" sign in 2007, it was rescued by the Devil's Rope & Route 66 Museum in nearby McLean, Texas. *Courtesy of Jim Ross*

Reptiles Galore, located east of McLean, Texas, was Mike Allred's final place of business. *John Margolies Roadside America Photograph Archive, Library of Congress*

that read: RATTLESNAKES! EXIT NOW.

Mike Allred's new enterprise was short-lived. In 1979 he had a fatal heart attack, and his snakes were gunny-sacked and transferred back to Addie in Alanreed. She continued to enthrall tourists well into the 1980s, making the Regal Reptile Ranch the last of the route's snake pits. Mike Allred's lofty RATTLESNAKES! sign, along with a fabricated metal cobra used as a prop in Alanreed, were later acquired by the Route 66 Museum in McLean, Texas.

* * *

Herman Atkinson, fresh out of the military in 1946, was inspired by his older brother Jake to follow in his footsteps. Jake owned the Rattlesnake Trading Post at Bluewater, New Mexico, a formidable building that also housed a reptile garden, café, and bar. Herman and his wife, Phyllis, set up shop as the Lost Canyon Trading Post in Milan, just west of Grants, beginning with a small animal zoo and two boa constrictors. The snakes were the spark, and by 1948 they had expanded, changed the name to Cobra

Cobra Gardens in Milan, New Mexico, was the king of snake farms in the early 1950s. *66postcards.com*

Maude Michael, Virginia Barnes, Ina Norman, and Emily Ross at Cobra Gardens, 1952. *Photo by and courtesy of Curt Norman*

Gardens, and were caretakers to over 300 ophidians, including a large collection of cobras. In only eight years, Cobra Gardens grew to become the largest and most successful reptile farm on the route, utilizing 44 billboards during its peak years and drawing thousands of visitors annually.

It was a family affair, with youngsters Peter and Marilynn Atkinson handling large but docile snakes to thrill tourists. Herman became self-schooled in herpetology, learning enough about reptiles to properly care for them and to educate visitors. One of their premier attractions was a Sumatran cobra that had been owned by Grace Wiley of California, acquired after she was fatally bitten during a photo shoot for *TRUE* magazine.

In 1953, the Atkinsons decided to sell out and move to Scottsdale, Arizona, where they opened another trading post. Their snakes were sold to the Rattle Snake Trading Post, by then under new ownership, and the former Cobra Gardens became the more modest Cactus Gardens. Herman Atkinson died in 2009, followed by Phyllis three years later. Most of the Cobra Gardens building was demolished in 2011, but faded graphics from its days as Cactus Gardens are still visible on remaining walls.

* * *

A deeper story is that of Two Guns in eastern Arizona. As tourist traps go, it had no equal. Within the ruins of the sprawling stone complex there lies a multi-layered history of intrigue, homicide, and mystery spanning the better part of a century.

Perched on the rim of rugged Canyon Diablo 20 miles west of Winslow, Two Guns originated in 1922 when Earl and Louise

Rimmy Jim Giddings (at right) at Two Guns, Arizona, circa 1930. *66postcards.com*

Harry "Indian" Miller of Two Guns fame. *Drawing © Shellee Graham 2024*

Cundiff acquired 320 acres along the National Old Trails Road where it crossed the canyon and opened a store and restaurant. They called it Canyon Lodge. The colorful and mischievous "Rimmy" Jim Giddings built a Texaco station there, but left in 1933 to open a new place on the route near Meteor Crater. Giddings carried a six-gun, was known to prank tourists, and claimed to have a graveyard out back for salesmen.

In 1925, Harry "Indian" Miller (1879–1951) signed a 10-year lease with the Cundiffs to operate a museum and curio shop in partnership with Joe "Yellowfeet" Secakuku (1895–1970), a Hopi Indian chief from the Second Mesa. Miller had served in the Spanish-American War, and then in the Philippines, where he remained until 1914. While there, he married Ena Oloan and fathered three of their four children. Though Caucasian, Miller assumed the persona of an Apache Indian upon his return to the states and identified as such throughout his adult life. He spent some time in the San Diego area and then migrated to Indiana, where his last child was born. He and Ena then divorced, and in 1923 he married Margaret Hamlet. They relocated to Arizona, where Harry managed a museum and zoo at Walnut Canyon National Monument prior to settling at Two Guns.

Both Miller and Secakuku had reputations—Miller as a trader and artist, and Secakuku as a wood carver and dancer who had

Map showing the relationship of the Two Guns, Arizona, complex and US 66. *Courtesy of Jim Ross and Shellee Graham*

Chief Joe Secakuku in 1924.
Authors' Collection

Author Gladwell Richardson.
Cline Library, Northern Arizona University

been master of Indian Ceremonies at the Grand Canyon's El Tovar Hotel. They named their new attraction Fort Two Guns, supposedly derived from Miller's admiration of silent film star William "Two Guns" Hart. Miller, now calling himself "Chief Crazy Thunder," added a zoo behind his museum and opened a cave located in the canyon as tourist attractions.

The tale of the cave dates to 1878, as told in *Two Guns, Arizona*, a 1968 nonfiction book by prolific western writer Gladwell Richardson (1903–1980). Richardson, both a novelist and western historian, published the story in article form in 1967 for both the *Arizona Republic* newspaper and *Big West* magazine. His family owned Two Guns from 1950 to 1962.

According to Richardson, an Apache raid in June 1878 left 50 men, women, and children killed in Navajo villages at Newberry and Gasden Mesas, along with three children kidnapped. In response, Navajo warriors led by B'ugoettin, Redshirt, and Hosteen Natani gave chase but failed to cut off their escape. After a second raid the following day, scouts Nahe and B'ugoettin Begay (the elder's son) discovered the Apaches' hideout in the Canyon Diablo cave. An arriving Navajo war party built a fire at the cave's entrance, and the 42 trapped Apaches and their horses all suffocated. Richardson noted that an 1892 area earthquake collapsed a land bridge that partially blocked the cave's entrance and altered its interior.

Nearly a half-century later, Harry Miller comes along, reportedly hires Hopi Indians to clear horse and human bones from the cave, adds electric lights and fake cliff dwelling walls inside, and begins conducting tours of his "Mystery Cave," as Richardson initially referred to it. In a real photo postcard published before Miller left there in 1931, the cave appears as "Apache Caves," presumably the name it was given by Miller. It is not yet known how, or exactly when, it became "Apache Death Cave."

Both Richardson's book and the *Arizona Republic* article list multiple sources, including statements made by Harry Miller as well as family members of Navajos involved in the raid, along with their photos. In spite of these attributions, Richardson's account is the only known record of the massacre, and he also has been accused by at least one historian of greatly exaggerating the story

Postcard advertising the Apache Caves at Two Guns, circa 1930.
Steve Rider Collection

The original Two Guns Zoo was on the canyon rim behind Indian Miller's museum and residence.
Authors' Collection

Indian Miller with visitors, date unknown. The zoo was reached through the portal behind him.
66postcards.com

of the Canyon Diablo railroad camp just three miles north of Two Guns. While this opens the door to doubt, lack of corroborating evidence for the Apache raid or embellishment of an unrelated story do not necessarily render the Two Guns tale fiction. The word "Apache" may have been chosen by Indian Miller because of his assumed identity, or it could be that the story of the raid existed long before Richardson wrote about it. Until more evidence surfaces, it remains a mystery.

Indian Miller was a natural roadside entrepreneur, and his future shined until landlord Earl Cundiff's temper cost him his life at the hands of Miller on March 3, 1926. Tension between the two had been percolating for weeks, reaching the point where Miller's wife, Margaret, allegedly part Mohawk Indian, temporarily retreated to her family home in Rochester, New York. Cundiff, known to go around half-cocked, reportedly had accused Joe Secakuku of coddling his wife, Louise, and Indian Miller of burglarizing his store.

On the day of his death, Cundiff came to Miller's residence. Miller, in the midst of changing clothes, came out and the two talked, according to witnesses Joe Secakuku and two bystanders—A. J. Brite and his son, Archie. They stated that Cundiff then left, but several minutes later shots rang out from inside Miller's dwelling. The three men reasoned that Cundiff had entered Miller's residence, which was adjacent to the museum, by sneaking along the canyon rim behind the stone wall there. Miller was arrested, charged with murder, and denied bail.

At the highly publicized trial in Flagstaff, both sides had supporters. Miller's testimony stated that Cundiff confronted him, snatched his .38 pistol from a table, and fired just as Miller pushed the weapon aside, the bullet punching a hole through Miller's shirt. A scuffle ensued, Miller ended up with the gun, and Cundiff was shot dead. The three men outside rushed to the scene and found Miller standing over Cundiff's body. "I had to do it," Miller stated. There were no eyewitnesses.

Newspapers reported that Earl Cundiff had a history of assault, verbal abuse, battery, and threats with a firearm, including brandishing a gun at Joe Secakuku's family inside Joe's curio shop. The county sheriff testified to Cundiff's numerous arrests. The *Williams News* reported that the 40-year-old was a tragic character "dangerously deranged" from falls he suffered during World War I, and that he had "an increasing homicidal tendency" for which institutionalization was being sought. Miller, on the other hand,

Ruins of the original Two Guns Zoo behind Indian Miller's residence, 2018.
Courtesy of Jim Ross

Harry Edgar Miller was born to Henry Harrison Miller of Iowa and Sara A. Rice of Missouri, both Caucasian pioneers of European descent. He is pictured here with his second wife Margaret and his four children by first wife Ena Oloan: May, Lulu, Ben, and Kentis. *Courtesy of Cathy Loren McKay*

The often-photographed entrance to the "new" zoo, as it appeared in 1991. The original Two Guns complex, across the canyon, is visible in the background. *Courtesy of Shellee Graham*

was described as an even-tempered man who abhorred violence.

It didn't help the Cundiff camp that Miller testified with poise and confidence, frustrating prosecutor Frank Harrison to the point that he demanded of Miller, "You think you are smart, don't you?" To which Miller replied, "No, you are smart. I am intelligent." The verdict was not guilty.

Miller resumed operations, but bad blood persisted. His highway billboards were vandalized. Miller was subsequently charged with defacing Cundiff's tombstone, which had been inscribed, "Killed by Indian Miller." In 1930, Louise Cundiff, now married to Louis Hayes, sued Miller over the terms of his lease. Tiring of it all, in 1931 Miller moved to the Cave of the Seven Devils near Lupton.

By 1934, Louise Cundiff was married to her third husband, Phillip Hesch. When construction of a new Route 66 alignment began in the late 1930s, they were forced to reestablish Two Guns on the north side of the Canyon Diablo bridge. Gladwell Richardson's father, S. I. Richardson, bought it in 1950, and in 1959 passed it on to Gladwell and his siblings. They sold it in 1962 to Ida Rawlinson, who in turn sold it in 1963 to Ben Dreher. A devastating fire in 1971 caused Dreher to walk away. The property has since had other owners, but remains a ruin.

Following Miller's departure from Two Guns, Joe Secakuku continued to run his curio shop for several years with wife Adiah, a Harvey Girl he had married while at El Tovar. Along with his brother Hale, they also owned stores in Flagstaff, Williams, and

The Two Guns station and zoo were relocated to another bend in the canyon when the route moved in 1940. *Authors' Collection*

other locations. Harry "Indian" Miller died on December 19, 1951, at his Lupton home, and is buried in Gallup's Hillcrest Cemetery. Chief Joe died of cancer in 1970.

Among the countless versions of the Two Guns story, no two are alike. Inarguable is that until it was vacated, Two Guns at times had generated dark energy. The Cundiff store mysteriously burned in 1929, three years after Earl Cundiff was killed by Miller. In 1931, Indian Miller was viciously mauled at his zoo by a mountain lion and hospitalized. Ben Dreher's Two Guns ownership was terminated by a massive fire.

Navajos allegedly warned both Miller and Cundiff that Canyon Diablo was cursed. True or not, it is said that for years after the massacre, traders who camped there were often awakened by the wails of dying Apaches riding the night wind.

Ruins of the second Two Guns Zoo, looking toward the back side of the entrance. *Courtesy of Jim Ross*

Bloody 66

LABELS TEND to stick. Along the route, evocative tags such as "Deadman's Curve" or "Suicide Bridge" hold like welded iron. Once a fatal accident is repeated, the location is assigned the blame, even if the fault belongs to drivers. Fair or not, the number of deadly wrecks at various spots during the highway's existence engendered the stigma "Bloody 66."

Accidents are as certain as the daily sunrise. Even with today's sophisticated safety features, lessons are still learned. Cars can withstand only so much impact, and deadly intersections often remain unfixed until a body count demands attention. Impaired drivers guarantee collisions, as do missing, damaged, unreadable, or inadequate road signs. Animals and other hazards wait in ambush, and distractions loom large. A simple sideways glance at the wrong moment can kill or maim. Brakes fail and tires explode. Lives forever change in the blink of an eye.

In the early days of motoring, speed limits were defined as "reasonable and proper." Paved roads had no center lines, passing on hills was unrestricted, curves were often sharp and shoulders soft. Changes came with money, but it took time.

Throughout the pre-interstate era, politicians ascended their pulpits to champion more funding, often using colorful language. A Missouri state senator in 1954 theatrically declared that sections of Route 66 between Rolla and Lebanon "ooze and drip with blood." This, of course, was only one notorious stretch. Others included Glenrio to Tucumcari, New Mexico, and Holbrook to Winslow, Arizona. Virtually every state laid claim to a stable of "dead man's" curves.

In truth, blame was shared. Until the 1960s, most vehicles had metal dashboards and no seatbelts. Even the heavy-gauge steel of bloated Detroit sedans crumpled like cheap tin cans when hit. Curves often appeared with

Elimination of railroad grade crossings was an ongoing priority in making the route safer. This unfortunate collision took place in St. Louis, Missouri.
Authors' Collection

In August 1953, a tire blew out on a car pulling a trailer as this bus attempted to pass, causing a collision that sent both vehicles plunging into Deer Creek just west of Hydro, Oklahoma, killing six and injuring 35.
Oklahoma Department of Transportation

Commemorative marker identifying Dead Man's Curve in Towanda, Illinois.
Courtesy of Pat Bremer

little warning and roadways undulated through rolling hills. Those on a budget often motored straight through to avoid lodging expenses, sometimes at the cost of their lives. A 1962 study by the Arizona Highway Patrol revealed that nearly half of 1961 Route 66 fatalities were non-collision accidents and that half of those were caused by fatigue.

Segments known as "Bloody 66" were a byproduct of faster cars and the failure of improvements to keep pace with increased traffic. For the most part, these death zones fed on the bodies of those who were distracted, speeding, drunk, negligent, or nodding off. Passengers and the occupants of cars they crashed into added to the carnage. Not unlike the stain a heinous crime leaves on an idyllic small town, the "Bloody 66" label detracts from the romance of the road, but it serves as another reminder that getting your kicks on Route 66 can lead to an unexpected and tragic ending.

This forsaken café in Essex, California, was left six miles from the nearest I-40 exit. *Courtesy of Jim Ross*

CHAPTER 9

Bypass

IT WAS A WORD that struck fear and anger into hearts and minds. *Bypass.* No interpretation was needed, and it resulted in only two outcomes: time saved for through traffic and hardship for everyone else. The burn of bypass had been felt in the route's early years but was largely accepted once uniform paving was completed. It gnashed its teeth again in the 1940s, particularly in Illinois, where city business districts were circumvented by two-lane and, later, four-lane realignments. In 1953, Oklahomans witnessed the first multi-county bypass with the opening of the Turner Turnpike between Tulsa and Oklahoma City, a project that foretold the future of the entire route.

Ribbon-cutting ceremony for the Turner Turnpike in 1953. *Oklahoma Department of Transportation*

President Dwight D. Eisenhower, elected in 1952, was keen on infrastructure. Having seen the Autobahn in Germany during the war, he was a willing partner in upgrading the nation's transportation system. In 1956 he signed the National Interstate and Defense Highways Act, authorizing $25 billion for 42,500 miles of superhighways. Less than a decade later, replacement of US 66 by five emerging interstates was underway: I-55 in Illinois, I-44 through Missouri and eastern Oklahoma, I-40 from Oklahoma City west to Barstow, California, and I-15 and I-10 from Barstow to Santa Monica.

Dual signage on interstates was a common sight as US 66 was gradually replaced. *66postcards.com*

Spotty interstate construction required motorists to jump back and forth from US 66. *Missouri Department of Transportation*

The elaborate and popular Stony Dell Pool at Arlington, Missouri, was lost to I-44. *Authors' Collection*

For the next 20 years the Mother Road was sliced, diced, realigned, and otherwise maltreated in a slow, methodical dismemberment. As stretches of super-slab opened to traffic, US 66 signs were moved onto the interstate, disrupting the route's continuity and forcing motorists to shift from one to the other. Only those sections safely separated from interstate corridors maintained their integrity for the duration.

Countless businesses, houses, barns, pastures, and the like were wiped out by the intrusive new highways. Small villages such as Lela, Texas, and Cuervo, New Mexico, were literally cut in half, never to recover. Four-lane sections of US 66 were upgraded to interstate standards. Two-lane stretches were retained for interstate service roads where feasible; otherwise, they were excavated or designated for county or local use, with leftovers deeded to connecting landowners. In spite of it all, when the screech and clank of the bulldozers finally ended, the majority of the route, minus its signage, was still drivable in one incarnation or another.

* * *

Though doomed, US 66 did not go quietly. As early as 1958 officials from Arizona traveled to Washington, DC, to protest interstate construction standards. Other citizens there formed a "No Bypass Committee" and promoted it across the state. Their goal was to hold the Bureau of Public Roads to its stated intent: to focus on

I-44 construction at Springfield, Missouri, in 1959. US 66 at the time was on Kearney Street, visible as an east-west four-lane south of the interstate. *USGS Earth Explorer*

rural areas and avoid bypasses until requested by city officials. Meanwhile, small communities route-wide were already fighting the threat, fully aware of the impending peril.

News reporting picked up as projects got underway. A June 28, 1962, *Daily Oklahoman* headline read: "Chop U.S. 66 Into Five Interstate Markings? What a Horrible Idea!" Similar reactions and efforts to slow or stop the advance varied considerably from state to state.

In Illinois, I-55 was essentially another layer of bypass and met comparatively little resistance. A significant portion of the route in Missouri had been widened to four lanes by the late 1950s, and most of that was simply modified to meet limited-access standards. Kansas and its three Route 66 communities suffered the consequences of being left high and dry more than five miles from interstate traffic. In eastern Oklahoma, the route had enough separation from the Will Rogers and Turner Turnpikes (I-44) to

With completion of the interstates, some existing sections of four-lane US 66 were reduced to two lanes, cutting maintenance costs in half.
Courtesy of Shellee Graham

keep its designation, but traffic counts fell dramatically. In western Oklahoma, accusations of favoritism were avoided by an agreement requiring that all bypasses there open simultaneously. This was small consolation, but it was all they got.

In Texas, downtown Shamrock was positioned on US 83 almost a mile south of its intersection with US 66, which limited its economic loss to the city's northern edge. Given the size of Amarillo, I-40 construction there was relatively pain free. Lela, McLean, Alanreed, Groom, Conway, Vega, and Adrian, on the other hand, received only exits and have struggled since.

The real war was fought farther west, with New Mexico digging its heels in

Established in 1924, Eisler Bros. Old Riverton Store (now Nelson's) survived bypass and became a Mother Road icon during the renaissance.
Courtesy of Jim Ross

Sayre, Oklahoma, in the 1940s bustled with traffic. These days, only a sprinkling of cars will be found on Main Street there.
Authors' Collection

deepest. Dissent in the Land of Enchantment was such that in March 1963 Governor Jack Campbell signed legislation prohibiting the bypass of any town under 50,000 population without the consent of local officials. Except for Albuquerque and Roswell, this covered the entire state. An *Albuquerque Journal* headline on March 22 read: "Bypass Law May Halt All Road Projects." The law's implementation occurred even as projects skirting Budville and San Fidel were in progress, causing a work stoppage.

New Mexico's effort appeared courageous but lacked meat on the bone, as the BPR maintained leverage. They could, and did, withhold funding. The real intent of the legislation was to give communities a voice in gaining access to the interstates, but it accomplished little. Delays resulted, and in-state opponents voiced safety concerns, citing 17 fatalities in three years on a section of US 66 east of Grants.

Newspaper reports on this David-versus-Goliath standoff were mixed. One *Albuquerque Journal* article pointed out the seriousness of having more than $30 million in construction funds at stake. A follow-up piece was titled, "Anti-Bypass Law Most Revolutionary in U.S." It listed McCartys, Moriarty, Tucumcari, and Santa Rosa as communities on the route having rejected bypasses. Predictably, only nine months along, legislative opposition took root. In 1965 the law was modified, lowering the population threshold requiring approval, and in 1966 it was repealed. The fight continued, but victory was found only in getting exits where none were planned.

California took on the BPR as well. Most of the route there crossed the barren Mojave Desert before reaching San Bernardino and the heavily populated Los Angeles County. Elsewhere, Barstow and Victorville were big enough to cope, as was Needles on the state's eastern border. Sacrificing the desert hamlets of Goffs, Essex, Chambless, Amboy, and Ludlow was accepted as unpreventable. Not acceptable was a late decision to relocate the interstate more than 40 miles north of Needles.

In 1965, BPR chief Rex Whitton announced plans to alter the course of I-40, then in progress at Kingman, Arizona. It was to be rerouted northwesterly to a crossing of the Colorado River above the Davis Dam and then west through Searchlight, Nevada, to join I-15 at Wheaton Springs, California. The rationale was that it would eliminate 100 miles of unnecessary interstate highway. Appalled, California Governor Edmund Brown appealed directly to President Lyndon Johnson, pointing to previously approved 1960 plans under Whitton's predecessor, B. D. Tallamy, as well as construction of the Colorado River bridge east of Needles, already underway. The ruckus wasn't settled until the spring of 1966, when Undersecretary of Transportation Alan S. Boyd overruled the BPR's Whitton, citing solid and convincing reasons in a congressional hearing.

By 1973, discontinuous sections of interstate still decorated the land as work progressed. Bypassing the loop through Amboy, California, required bisecting the Bristol Mountains a dozen miles north of the existing route. The railroad sought new tracks there as well, and the solution agreed upon was to use atom bombs. It was named Project Carryall, and called for substituting 23 nuclear devices for dynamite. In the end, conventional blasting was used after further study requested by the Atomic Energy Commission indefinitely delayed construction. It was a bizarre chapter in the story of the route, one in which the potential long-term negative effects of excavating with nukes were avoided.

As elsewhere, small communities in Arizona were cast aside like road hazards, with Williams the last to go. It has been said that officials there managed to keep traffic funneled along city streets until 1984 through clever legal maneuvering, but this was not the

Except for a fuel stop and a motel/café near the interstate exit, Ludlow, California, is now a ghost town.
Courtesy of Jim Ross

Even with an I-40 exit nearby, this station near San Fidel, New Mexico, could not survive the emergence of interstate truck stops. *Courtesy of Jim Ross*

In the 1950s, Rocky's offered fuel, food, liquor, and towing services. *Authors' Collection*

case. Proposed plans for the bypass were first presented there by the highway department in October 1975. In the spring of 1976 it was reported that work would begin in early 1977 and finish in 1979. Plans were approved, but right-of-way acquisition caused further delay, and in late 1979 the Arizona DOT sued a group of landowners who refused to accept already-agreed-to compensation.

Early in 1980, bids were finally sought for the first phase of the Williams bypass. Completion was scheduled for 1982, but this didn't play out. The contractor, Tanner Construction, stopped work in the fall of that year. At issue was a requirement to use a new asphaltic mix for paving, one that Tanner claimed came without the formula specifications. A lawsuit ensued, leading to a 56-day trial in 1983. In court, State Attorney General lawyers Joe Acosta Jr. and Richard Kamps, apparently lean on compelling evidence, blamed God and President Reagan. God was responsible, they asserted, for weather delays, and the economy was at fault for influencing Tanner to submit an overly aggressive low bid, which they claimed the company now sought to void. Superior Court Judge Morris Rozar ruled in favor of Tanner, and they were released from their contract.

In May 1984, Corn Construction of Grand Junction, Colorado, won the contract to finish the Williams bypass and promised to do so before the end of the year. They beat their deadline, opening I-40 for traffic on Monday, October 8. On October 13, a ribbon-cutting ceremony was held at the Grand Canyon Avenue I-40 exit. The event included a parade, a car show, and a performance of "Get Your Kicks on Route 66" by composer and guest of honor Bobby Troup, followed by a street dance. Troup, aware of the event's significance and somewhat saddened by it, later expressed wonder at the celebration, suggesting the occasion should have been conducted more like a wake.

Williams could afford to celebrate. They were given three exits and had the Grand Canyon Railroad as a tourist draw to compensate. Elsewhere, when the traffic spigot was cranked shut, small communities without other advantages became ghost towns or were left gasping for economic air. Some abandoned their downtown districts and re-centered around interstate exits, hoping to hang on. Others limped along as best they could. Businesses between towns where no exits existed were soon shuttered.

Hit hard and left bitter were Helen and Nyal "Rocky" Rockwell in eastern Arizona. Their Old Stage Station, located just outside the Petrified Forest National Park, began life in the 1800s as a stagecoach stop. The Rockwells bought the property in 1954 and ran a service station, café, and towing service there. Business was good, but not for long. A slight change in the highway's alignment in the late 1950s disrupted access. This was followed immediately by I-40 construction, which wiped out their buildings and left them isolated five miles from the nearest exit. Lawsuits followed, but in the end only the towing service was left as a source of income. In 1987 Rocky retired, after which he often greeted Route 66 explorers and told tales of his life on the highway. Helen passed away in 1995, followed by Nyal in 1998. He was 84. Now fenced off, the deserted remains of Rocky's Old Stage Station contain the garage, a couple of mobile homes, school buses, unsold used cars, and other junk strewn like litter hurled from interstate big rigs.

In Hydro, Oklahoma, Lucille Hamons watched helplessly as traffic in front of the station she had owned since 1941 sidestepped

Nyal and Helen Rockwell in retirement, 1994.
Courtesy of Jim Ross

The faded sign at the ruins of Rocky's Old Stage Station, 2021.
Courtesy of Jim Ross

Lucille's station, with living quarters overhead, faces south on a grassy knoll just outside Hydro, Oklahoma. Now preserved, it remains a favorite tourist stop. *Courtesy of Jim Ross*

Lucille Hamons at her induction into the Oklahoma Route 66 Hall of Fame in 1999.
Courtesy of Jim Ross

onto I-40, separating her from customers with a fence and a hundred feet of fairway. Adding salt to the wound, the westbound I-40 on-ramp was positioned just east of her store, siphoning away even vehicles that had used the Hydro exit. The year was 1967. Lucille had closed her four-unit motor court in 1962 following her divorce, and she was now forced to survive by selling beer, cigarettes, and convenience items to locals and to college students in nearby Weatherford. For the next 34 years she persevered, ultimately earning recognition as a highway celebrity. This she fully embraced, often spinning yarns for an hour or more with a single visitor and posing for countless photographs. Lucille Hamons never remarried and never retired, keeping her place open until the day she died in August 2000 at age 85. Her station was listed on the National Register of Historic Places in 1997, and has since been preserved. The Hamons Court neon sign is now on display at the Smithsonian's Museum of American History.

Most who found themselves sharing the fate of Rocky or Lucille were unable to recover, and as the final days of the route steadily approached, it was generally bemoaned by the press. In August 1981, the *Tucson Daily Star* ran a story with this headline: "Passport of Pavement That Symbolized Freedom and Dreams Is All But Gone." A related story explained that the interstate system was nearly completed after 23 years. That same month, the *Daily Oklahoman* featured a story under the banner, "Once Bustling U.S. 66 Now a Phantom Road West."

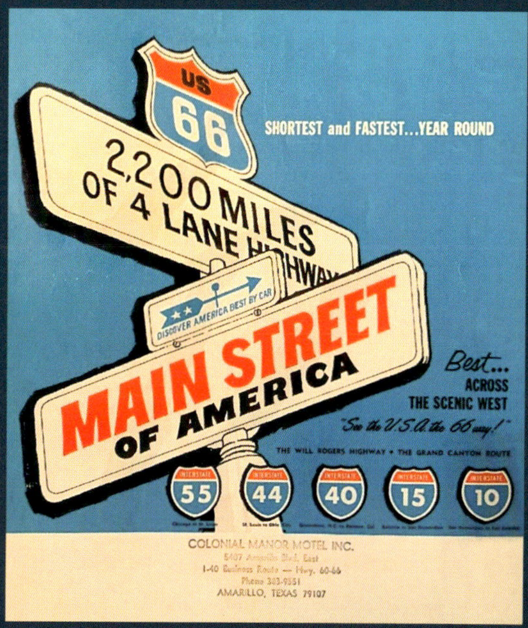

This 1970s association brochure displays its new name along with interstate emblems.
Kathy Anderson Collection

The US Highway 66 Association, like the named trails organizations of the 1920s, worked tirelessly to delay the inevitable, but the juggernaut could not be stopped. In 1970 the association's name was changed to the Main Street of America Association. Six years later, with only snippets of US 66 apart from the interstates still signed, and with its membership dissipated, the association disbanded. Official decertification of US 66 occurred at different times in different areas, but concluded less than a year after the 1984 Williams, Arizona, bypass.

Spans of Time

BEYOND THE RIVERBANK, slanted sunlight glints off water slithering through sandbars the color of cinnamon. Inside a parked car, a mother and her toddler peacefully doze, undisturbed by the sprinkle of autumn leaves swirling through the open windows. Except for the rattle of a busy woodpecker, only the occasional cough of a passing flivver interrupts the shaded quiet. At river's edge, another sluggish catfish is jerked into sunshine by a pole outfitted with twine and baited with bread. The fisherman grins in relief, as the unrelenting drought has put his family on the run and he can furnish no other supper. He regards the hulking iron bridge nearby, grateful for the company and the sense of safety it provides. They will eat heartily, camp with the bridge tonight, and face tomorrow when it comes.

* * *

Bridges symbolize strength. Their brawny beams allow motorists to imagine they share in the triumph of conquering obstacles. They serve as waypoints and fishing piers, a place to rendezvous, and offer shelter. Only the automobile and the locomotive are more emblematic of transportation history. From the days of Roman stone arches until the middle of the 20th century, bridges were culturally important. Like buildings, they were functional works of art limited in style only by the laws of physics. Diversity in materials and artistic flair rendered spans that quickly became engineering marvels, landmarks, and subjects for artists.

Today, limitations placed in the name of conformity and budgeting have stripped away aesthetics. With few exceptions, elegant arches and steel trusses have been replaced with generic grade-level beams and girders, rendering utilitarian spans that forego architectural eloquence for economical safe passage.

Initial paving of the route included hundreds of new bridges, combining steel and concrete into a wide array of designs. They were built for permanence, but poorly considered was the inevitable need to accommodate greater loads and larger vehicles. The result was that many of them became substandard long before expected.

Those still in use from the two-lane era rank high as photo subjects and points of interest, yet they are being lost with alarming frequency. Highway departments tend to neglect bridges that no longer meet standards,

The 1923 Big Piney River Bridge at Devils Elbow, Missouri, was successfully rehabbed in 2013 through a coordinated multi-county effort. *Courtesy of Shellee Graham*

The beautiful and ornate 1913 Colorado Street Bridge in Pasadena, California, underwent total rehabilitation in 1993 and remains in use. *Courtesy of Jim Ross*

Missouri's 1924 Niangua River Bridge was replaced in 2022 despite its historical significance. *Courtesy of Jim Ross*

allowing them to degrade until replacement is unavoidable. While some transportation officials now recognize the need for their preservation, saving these testaments to the past remains an uphill challenge.

The relatively few bridges now residing on private property are among the least vulnerable. For the rest, obsolescence leads to outcomes as varied as the structures themselves. The majority are destined for removal. Others continue in use, for now. Those closed to traffic have been either deeded to new owners, preserved, or allowed to remain in limbo. Saving as many as possible calls for continued vigilance and a willingness to champion their historic significance. How many survive the route's second century will depend on those efforts.

The Timber Creek Bridge on the I-40 service road west of Elk City, Oklahoma, is a rare modified Pratt through truss design that remains endangered. *Courtesy of Shellee Graham*

At three quarters of a mile in length and made up of 38 "pony" trusses on each side, the 1932 South Canadian River Bridge east of Bridgeport, Oklahoma, is unique to the route. It was successfully rehabbed in 2024. *Photo by Jim McCain*

Abandonment in the desert west of Leupp, Arizona, has helped preserve this 1930s bridge resting within eyesight of I-40. *Courtesy of Jim Ross*

The only surviving Marsh Arch Bridge on Route 66, between Riverton and Baxter Springs, Kansas, was saved in the 1990s after a long battle fought by the Kansas Route 66 Association. *Courtesy of Shellee Graham*

The shuttered Budville Trading Company, 2009. *Courtesy of Shellee Graham*

CHAPTER 10

Villains and Victims

OOD SOULS vastly outnumber bad souls. The downside to this favorable imbalance is that it leads to a sense of trust, permitting villains easy access to victims. No facet of society is exempt, even within criminal quarters. Likewise, the story of the route is peppered with the sting of dark deeds. Most of the robberies, kidnappings, and homicides that taint its history are long forgotten. Others, like the killing of Earl Cundiff by Indian Miller at Two Guns, Arizona, are connected with a known place or individual and continue to circulate.

Howard Neal "Bud" Rice fit that category. It was no secret that Bud had critics, but low marks for popularity had nothing to do with his death. In the mid-1940s, he opened a trading company, station, and towing service near Cubero, New Mexico. His father, Roscoe, owned a station five miles west at San Fidel. Bud's roadside complex, which included rental cabins, became Budville when proclaimed so by Rice once he became justice of the peace there. And so began a legacy of alleged corruption, scandal, and murder that left a permanent scar on this tiny township. As recently as 1995, a Budville tavern owner offered a probing reporter this advice: "If you want to live here, you mind your own business."

Flossie and Bud during happy times. *Courtesy of Debby Miller*

Bud's sister Genta at their father Roscoe's San Fidel station, circa 1933. *Photo courtesy of her son David Chapman*

Rice became known for charging high towing and repair fees and for fining traffic violators sums that even fellow magistrates called excessive. He claimed the fines were necessary given the ever-rising number of fatal accidents. On the flip side, supporters praised him for rescuing disabled vehicles regardless of the hour. Well-liked by friends and neighbors, he often supplied shoes to area children and performed other acts of kindness, revealing a softer side. This was possibly influenced by the death of his mother, Olivia, by her own hand in 1946, occurring only three months after the suicide of her son and Bud's brother Bert, a World War II Marine Corps veteran.

The end for Bud, 54, came on a shivery November night in 1967 when he and employee Blanche Brown, 81, were murdered inside the trading post during a robbery. Each had been shot twice. Bud's wife, Aurora "Flossie" Chavez Rice, was left tied up, and their housekeeper, Nettie Buckley, who went unnoticed by the killer, was found hiding in a closet. At a roadblock near Grants, police first arrested Larry Bunten, a sailor who fit the description. Flossie, still sedated, tentatively identified him, and the search by law enforcement was called off, even though Bunten had a solid alibi and passed both polygraph and truth serum tests. He was held for 18 days, allowing the real perpetrator to get away clean.

Larry Lee Travis's senior picture. *Courtesy of Dr. Ron Miller*

In early 1968, a jailhouse tip fingered a new suspect, 26-year-old criminal and drifter Billy Ray White of Alabama, along with accomplice Joseph V. Dean Jr. of Albuquerque. An eight-month manhunt ensued, earning White a place on the FBI's Ten Most Wanted list after it was learned that he was concurrently wanted for robbery and attempted murder in Metairie, Louisiana, and for robbery of the Pueblo Loan Co. in Albuquerque. He was nabbed in August 1968 in Wood River, Illinois. Dean was caught in California, and confessed to providing a car and a gun for White to use for robberies.

The trial took place in Los Lunas, New Mexico, in March 1969. Flossie Rice, inexplicably spared by the shooter, positively identified White as the man who tied her up, but the defense made hay of Flossie's earlier misidentification of Larry Bunten. Two jailbirds took the stand to alibi White. The only other witness, Nettie Buckley, had died of illness shortly before the trial. The jury chose to believe the felons and not Flossie Rice, who sobbed uncontrollably when the verdict acquitting Billy Ray White was read.

Charges against Dean were dropped. White, however, did not go free. He was convicted in Louisiana and sent to the state penitentiary at Angola. There, he became lovers with his cellmate, who later wrote of White's culpability in the Budville killings. On June 10, 1974, seven years after the murders and while being comforted by his grieving celly, Billy Ray White cut his wrists and bled out.

Flossie, 47, who was a divorcee when she married Bud in 1947, had remarried shortly before the trial, this time to local troublemaker Max Atkinson, 33, a former convict who stunned the court by attacking Billy Ray White during his trial. In 1971, Atkinson was shot and his brother Phillip killed in ambush at the trading post following a brawl at a Budville tavern. Two years later, Max Atkinson was gunned down by acquaintance Gus Raney at Raney's area ranch during an argument.

Lingering rumors that Flossie and Max had conspired to kill Bud Rice proved unfounded, as Atkinson was in an Arizona prison on the night of the murders. Flossie, who later married a fourth time to Obie Hall, died in 1994 without enduring further mayhem. The Budville Trading Company, now shuttered and deteriorating, stands as the only tangible reminder of the events that altered so many lives there so long ago.

* * *

Darrouzett, Texas, is as rural as it gets, stuck like a postage stamp to Hwy. 15 in the extreme north panhandle. Perryton is 30 miles west, and the border with Oklahoma's panhandle four miles north. An agricultural community of 350 die-hards, it was home to Larry Lee Travis, a 1965 graduate of Darrouzett High School. Larry had a brother, Clayton, and two sisters, Donette and Tanya. Those who knew Larry remember him as a quiet young man who was well liked but guarded his privacy.

Roxann Brownlee in 1966.
From the Adrian, Texas, high school yearbook

The family moved to the Route 66 town of Adrian, Texas, in 1966, where Larry's father Don pastored the United Methodist Church and where Travis met high school student Ruth Roxann Brownlee. She was one of seven children born to Roxie and Joe Brownlee, who owned a Texaco station in nearby Glenrio, also on the route at the New Mexico border. Larry and Roxann, as she preferred to be called, married in January 1970 when she was 19 and he 23. Initially they lived in Adrian, but later moved to Glenrio with their adopted son, Joe Don Travis.

Larry helped at the Brownlee Texaco and worked odd jobs to support his family, but when I-40 bypassed Glenrio in 1973, things got tough. In the fall of 1975, he leased a Standard station in Adrian from Don Morgan, who had closed it earlier that year. Larry had previously worked for Morgan at a Shell station there, and Morgan believed he could make a go of it. Larry's Pontiac Catalina was fit for the 20-mile commute, and by the time he celebrated his 29th birthday in January 1976, he had built up a good business.

Lewis Steven Powell of Grapevine, Texas, was born in 1953. He joined the navy following high school, and not long after his discharge committed a robbery that sparked a lethal crime spree. On March 4, 1976, he shot to death 50-year-old World War II veteran Clyde Franklin Helton in a park at North Lake, near Irving, Texas. Helton, who had formerly lived in the Route 66 city of Joplin, Missouri, owned a Conoco station in Irving. Powell pushed Helton's car into the lake, then fled into the Texas Panhandle. Three days later, on the evening of March 7, he pulled into the Standard station one mile east of Adrian at about 8:30 p.m. He entered the office and without hesitation fatally shot Larry Travis in the back of

Larry Travis's 1968 Pontiac Catalina.
Courtesy of Shellee Graham

his head with a .38 caliber pistol. Powell then removed the cash drawer from the register and drove away.

Tourists found Larry Travis minutes later, slumped over a bench next to the pay phone. A vague description of a car leaving the station initiated a three-state dragnet. The next day, near Raton, New Mexico, Powell fired three shots at a pickup truck after the two had passed each other several times. Police were called, and Powell was cornered outside Trinidad, Colorado, where he also fired on the arresting officers. He subsequently pleaded guilty to both murders and received two life sentences plus 40 additional years for shooting at the cops. Powell's motives were never explained. A sentencing technicality later led to his parole, but it was soon violated and he was returned to prison.

Joe Brownlee's station in Glenrio has been closed for decades, and the Standard station in Adrian where Larry Travis died no longer exists. Roxann Travis never remarried. She later bought a home in Amarillo, but has maintained the family residence behind her father's station. Following his death, Larry's 1968 Pontiac was brought home, where it remains parked in front of Brownlee's Texaco, frozen in time.

* * *

Not everyone on the wrong end of a gun was a victim. Irvin "Blackie" Thompson chose a criminal path at a young age. Born in 1893, he was first sentenced for auto theft in Oklahoma in 1920.

Blackie Thompson mug shot.
National Archives

In 1923, he robbed a bank while on parole and was sent back to prison, only to be temporarily released to serve as an informant in Oklahoma's now-famous Osage Indian murders case. While free, he robbed a Drumright, Oklahoma, bank and killed a police officer, earning him an immediate return to the state pen in McAlester. He escaped in 1933 but was soon back in the slammer for sticking up banks in Texas.

This time Thompson landed in the penitentiary at Huntsville under a sentence of death, for which he qualified under Texas law. There, he conspired with killers Raymond Hamilton and Joe Palmer to escape the death house, something never before done. As members of Clyde Barrow's gang, Hamilton and Palmer were on death row for killing guard M. J. Crowson during an escape from the Eastham Prison Farm during a January 1934 raid by Barrow.

The breakout from Huntsville took place on July 22, 1934, the same day John Dillinger was gunned down in Chicago. Three other inmates, Whitey Walker, Roy Johnson, and Charlie Frazier, were shot and captured during the breakout. Walker did not survive. In April 1935, Ray Hamilton was nabbed in a Fort Worth rail yard after police intercepted a letter to his sister. Joe Palmer was collared in a Paducah, Kentucky, cornfield in August, exhausted and penniless. The two were executed in Huntsville's electric chair back-to-back on May 10, 1935, with the unrepentant Palmer going first.

Gangster Blackie Thompson came up short in his gun battle with officers in Amarillo, Texas. *FBI Photo via Wikimedia Commons*

By then, Blackie Thompson was already dead, but not from the hotseat. On December 6, 1934, while holed up in Amarillo, Texas, his whereabouts were tipped to police, and they moved into position near his rented house. The cautious Blackie sensed trouble, and as he approached the house that evening in a stolen Ford V-8, he got jumpy and sped off. The chase was on, and it led to Route 66, heading east. Ten officers were in pursuit, but the Ford outdistanced them. It was a long-range rifle shot near the city limits that punctured a tire and sent the getaway car careening off the highway.

The standoff was brief. Police bullets blistered the roadway and shattered glass in Blackie's crippled sedan. Blackie lurched from the car with a shotgun and returned fire, but he was blinded by the glare of police headlights and was summarily ventilated by machine-gun slugs, struck 17 times before hitting the ground. Irvin Thompson's criminal career was finally over, ending on Route 66 in true gangster style. He was 41.

* * *

Toonerville was never more than a trading post and residence, planted on naked ground just east of Twin Arrows, Arizona. The name was almost certainly inspired by a comic strip that ran from 1908 to 1955 called Toonerville Folks. In the newspapers, the fictional

The Toonerville Trading Post in the 1950s. *Authors' Collection*

Toonerville had a Toonerville Trolley and was populated with Toonerfolks. They had names like Terrible-Tempered Truman and Little Woo-Woo Wortle. The feature enjoyed such popularity that urbanites began calling trolley cars "Toonervilles."

Despite its cartoon roots, there is nothing funny about events surrounding the Toonerville Trading Post. Originated by Earl Tinnin in the 1930s, the first tragic incident there occurred in 1947 when Earl's 14-year-old son George died after accidentally shooting himself in the head. In 1954, Tinnin sold the trading post to Merritt and Pearl McAlister. Seventeen years passed with no trouble. Then, around 1 p.m. on August 30, 1971, a man and a woman came in and ordered three hamburgers. Another man had stayed with the car outside. Pearl, 56, was at the grill when she was shot without warning in the side of her head. Merritt, 60, died instantly from a single shot to the heart while attempting to disarm Pearl's attacker. The assailants then demanded help opening the cash register from the semi-conscious Pearl. Inside was $70.

Pearl crawled to a phone and called her neighbor Joan Gray at Twin Arrows, who summoned police and then rushed to the scene with her husband, Charles. Merritt McAlister, a World War II veteran, had given up his habit of carrying a firearm on the premises. He still kept a list of license tags, but there had been no opportunity to record that of his killers. A dragnet failed to capture the thugs responsible, and the case went cold. It was reopened 43 years later in 2014, but remains unsolved. Pearl recovered and lived to be 84.

Route 66 advocate and preservationist Mary Smeal. *Courtesy of Ann Smeal*

In 1994, Toonerville became the residence of Mary Ellen Smeal, who purchased it from Henry and Nina Poore. Dr. Poore was the Flagstaff physician who had treated Pearl McAlister's gunshot wound. Mary, originally from Albuquerque, wore many hats. She was a Route 66 preservationist as well as comptroller at Northern Arizona University in Flagstaff and chief financial officer for the Hopi Tribal Economic Development Corporation. She was also the driving force behind efforts to restore and reopen the forsaken Twin Arrows Trading Post only a mile west of Toonerville. Her sense of compassion, kindness, and enthusiasm were infectious, endearing her to everyone she knew.

Efforts by Mary Ellen and the Hopi Tribe to revive Twin Arrows unfortunately ended when the Navajo Nation completed the Twin Arrows Casino on the opposite side of I-40 there in 2013. At nearby Toonerville, more trouble lurked. Mary's ex-husband, auctioneer Jeffery Owen Jones, gambled away proceeds from an auction, became a fugitive, was caught, and served jail time. Then, on November 16, 2016, he fatally shot 55-year-old Mary in her Toonerville home before turning the gun on himself in a cowardly act of murder-suicide that stunned the extended community.

The Toonerville Trading Post is currently owned by Mary's longtime friend Darla Jurrens. Giving up no secrets, it sits poker-faced next to I-40, its potential for continued misfortune unknown. Perhaps its history of tragedy is simple coincidence. Perhaps the combined spiritual energy of young George Tinnin, Merritt and Pearl McAlister, and Mary Ellen Smeal will bring lasting peace.

The Streamline Moderne Coral Court Motel in the early 1990s. *Courtesy of Shellee Graham*

The secretive John Carr, builder and owner of the Coral Court. *Authors' Collection*

The No-Tell Motel with a Touch of Class

JOHN CARR was possibly the most intimidating, charming, secretive, generous, and potentially dangerous character the route has known. Sparing no expense, in 1941 he built the Coral Court Motel, positioned on a pastoral sloping hillside studded with towering pin oaks. The eight-acre site was just west of the St. Louis city limits in the village of Marlborough, chosen purposely to keep issues with law enforcement manageable. From there he conducted "business" for the next 43 years.

Constructed in the Streamline Moderne style, Coral Court was an architectural masterpiece. Its artful curved walls, glass blocks, and glazed tile bricks delivered strong curb appeal. Each room had its own private garage, and Carr kept the grounds manicured. It was a success by any measure, yet how it was financed is unknown, and from the beginning it was tainted with mystery from the dark undercurrent surrounding its owner.

John Henry Carr was born in Uniontown, Pennsylvania, in 1901. He had been incarcerated at Leavenworth, Kansas, and was involved with prostitution. After the Detroit mob chased him out of Ohio, he migrated to St. Louis, where he ran at least one brothel. In 1946 Carr married former prostitute Jessie Hughes, possibly from his own stable of soiled doves. Carr was tall, with rugged good looks and piercing eyes. A friend described him as "dapper, orderly, handsome. He was a smooth talker and the king of control. He would have no trouble killing someone or having it arranged."

Outwardly, the Coral Court maintained a family atmosphere during the pre-interstate era. *Courtesy of Nell Ruth Young*

John Carr's Leavenworth Penitentiary mug shot from 1933. *National Archives*

Curved walls and glass blocks were a distinctive feature of the Coral Court. *St. Louis County Department of Parks & Recreation, Esley Hamilton Photo*

By appearances, the Coral Court was a family-oriented motel catering to tourists, and its occupancy rate was high. Less apparent was that it secretly percolated with illegal gambling and call-girl activity. There was at least one underground room and an escape tunnel disguised as a storm drain. It was generally known that Carr carried the Marlborough police department in his hip pocket.

In September 1953, headlines erupted with the kidnapping of 6-year-old Bobby Greenlease, son of a wealthy Kansas City Cadillac dealer, who was snatched by bumbling, alcoholic amateur criminals Carl Austin Hall and Bonnie Heady. They killed the child, buried him

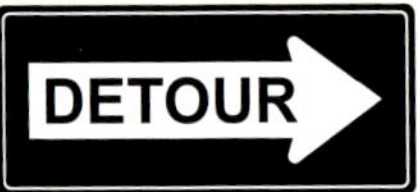

in Heady's back yard, and then drove to St. Louis after collecting $600,000 in ransom. The night of their arrival, Hall's reckless flashing of money in front of a cab driver prompted a tipoff to the cab company's owner, mobster Joe Costello. Hall's next mistake was renting a room at the Coral Court. The following day, Hall and Heady were conveniently arrested by officer Elmer Dolan and corrupt St. Louis police lieutenant Lou Shoulders, who had ties to both Costello and John Carr. Approximately half of the ransom money was never recovered, and many still believe that Shoulders, Costello, and Carr were the beneficiaries. Detective Shoulders and officer Dolan went to prison for perjury in the case, but evidence against Carr was lacking. Hall and Heady confessed, waived their right to appeal, and were executed side by side in the Missouri State Penitentiary's gas chamber on December 18, 1953, just 29 days after sentence was passed.

Greenlease kidnappers Carl Austin Hall and Bonnie Heady.
Missouri Department of Corrections

Kidnap victim Bobby Greenlease with his father.
St. Louis Mercantile Library Collections, University of Missouri, St. Louis

According to Carr's grandson John Dover, "My grandfather was the type of person who would pull out his wallet and hand $500 to a complete stranger that he felt bad about." Motel staff also spoke of his kindness and generosity. On the flip side, Carr was not one to cross. St. Louis reporter John Auble once stated that "(Carr) had close ties with Buster Wortman, the mafia boss from East St. Louis. He had an underground room where he played cards with hoodlums, most notably Bugsy Seigel."

Bookings declined with the construction of I-44 in the early 1970s, foretelling the end for Coral Court. "No-tell" clients increased, and the motel's reputation became more sullied. Carr continued its operation until his death in 1984, taking his secrets and the motel's future to the grave. Jessie remarried, but no effort was made to resuscitate the motel. It closed in 1993, and while preservationists made a gallant effort to save it, it was knocked down for a condo project in 1995. On orders from Jessie Carr, even the sign was destroyed. She died a year later. By arrangement with the contractor, one bungalow was dismantled and reassembled at the National Museum of Transportation in St. Louis, such was the motel's significance. Coral Court has since been the subject of a play, a book, and a documentary film.

Preserved sections of the motel's stone entrance walls are the only evidence of its former presence. They stand along Watson Road like misplaced headstones. Even though it is gone, the Coral Court remains one of the route's most revered icons—a jewel of the road whose notoriety was made possible only through a fated collision of architectural style and the enigmatic John Carr.

I have many, many memories. It broke my heart to see 'em tear it down.
Anonymous, St. Louis, Missouri

I admired its architecture, if not its bedsprings.
S. L., St. Louis, Missouri

This is a place for St. Louisans to be proud of? I think not. It's a dark, sleazy place with bad memories. I'll be glad when it's gone.
Marie in Fenton, Missouri

The Coral Court Motel was a unique place that could be naughty and nice at the same time and retain a sense of innocence. Now that's a true landmark!
Joe Edwards, owner, Blueberry Hill, St. Louis, Missouri

Jessie Hughes Carr. *Authors' Collection*

Demolition of the Coral Court generated significant publicity. *Courtesy of Shellee Graham*

Carthage, Missouri's Boots Court became a shining star of the renaissance, undergoing a two-phase renovation under two different owners. *Courtesy of Tim Anderson*

CHAPTER 11

Renaissance

MBLEMS WERE expunged from maps and signs yanked from poles. Parts of it became privately owned or were buried beneath the interstates. The rest was concealed behind a basketful of unfamiliar names and numbers, stripped of identity and dispatched to history. US 66 was no more. Except that it could not be purged from the popular imagination and, despite official decree, almost all of the route still existed in one incarnation or another.

November 11, 1926, until June 26, 1985. Fifty-eight years, seven months, 15 days. For the country's most famous highway, its lifespan was remarkably short. Removal of its remaining shields signaled that something special had been lost, and a tinge of anxiety swirled through the nation's

Removal of US 66 signs in Joplin, Missouri, 1985. *Missouri Department of Transportation / Color by Shellee Graham*

In Clinton, Oklahoma, the state's first shield to be auctioned is put up for bid. *Oklahoma Historical Society*

Angel & Vilma's Route 66 Gift Shop in Seligman, Arizona, remains a magnet for tourists. *Courtesy of Jim Ross*

consciousness like nostalgic haze. Even highway departments felt it. Instead of recycling US 66 highway markers, they held public auctions. Bidders swarmed to snatch them up, knowing their value was far greater than the dollars spent to own them. With its youthful demise, the route had carved a final notch in its pistol grip of legend.

Route 66 spent two decades on a respirator before the final day of reckoning. It had been dismantled randomly and excised from state highway systems at different times as requests from various states were submitted to AASHTO (the American Association of State Highway and Transportation Officials, formerly AASHO). California truncated the route in 1964 from Santa Monica back to Pasadena, and in 1974 it was stricken from their roster of US highways completely. On June 25, 1974, Missouri decertified the route from its border with Illinois all the way to Joplin; there, I-44 signs directed those wishing to follow US 66 into Oklahoma to exit and proceed west through Kansas to connect. Illinois pulled its US 66 shields in January 1977, and removal in Texas took place in July 1979. Oklahoma officially decertified the route with highway commission action on April 1, 1985. Remaining segments elsewhere were scissored out by the AASHTO Numbering Committee less than three months later, on June 26, 1985.

Lingering sentiments led to discussions by various groups of how to best commemorate

Seligman, Arizona's Snow Cap is a core feature of the city's comeback. *Courtesy of Tim Anderson*

the route. But it was those most adversely affected who picked up their shovels and began the exhumation. Barber and pool hall owner Angel Delgadillo had stewed about it since his hometown of Seligman, Arizona, was bypassed in September 1978, staring in disbelief the day traffic vanished behind an invisible slammed door. The town suffered a second hammer blow six years later when passenger rail service there was discontinued. In 1985, Seligman-based railroad employees were relocated. The whirlpool swirled, but Angel Delgadillo didn't give up. Instead, in a last-ditch effort to save the town, he rallied support to transform his small city into a roadside attraction.

In early 1987 the Historic Route 66 Association of Arizona was born in Seligman. Seven other states would follow this lead. With its remote location and a population of less than 1,000, Seligman was ideally positioned for what Angel had in mind, and his vision paid quick dividends. Businesses switched their focus to those with a thirst for days gone by, and traffic picked up. In 1988 they hosted the first annual Arizona Fun Run car cruise, establishing their city as a Mother Road destination. Adding icing to the cake, Delgadillo and the association successfully petitioned the state to designate parts of the Arizona route a Scenic Byway. With these acts, Seligman became an economic boomtown and set an example for the entire route.

By 1991, associations existed in all eight states, their mission to promote and preserve the route and to serve as a resource for travelers. The first documentary book, *Route 66: The Highway and Its People*, was published in 1988 by Susan Croce Kelly and Quinta Scott. Californian Tom Snyder formed the US Route 66 Association and in 1990 published the first guidebook for travelers. But it was the 1990 publication of *Route 66: The Mother Road* by Pulitzer Prize-nominated author Michael Wallis, coupled with a well-publicized book tour, that aroused national interest and kicked the revival into overdrive. A year later, the *Mother Road Journal*, a tabloid-style quarterly, premiered and gained wide readership. 1992 was the 66th anniversary of the route, generating multiple events and additional publicity. In 1993, *Route 66 Magazine* debuted, and in 1994 the National Historic Route 66 Federation was founded with preservation as its primary goal.

The book that brought national attention to the rebirth of the route.
Courtesy of Shellee Graham

Poster publicizing the first national roadie gathering in 1996.
Authors' Collection

An immediate challenge for enthusiasts was *finding* the route. With no road signs or maps depicting the mostly anonymous and sometimes discontinuous highway, guesswork often had to serve. Initial guides were basic and faulty. Records were scattered piecemeal across the archives of eight state highway departments, almost none of it cataloged. Research efforts by fledgling route historians were salted with mistakes soon repeated.

Unlike today, the world was not at the tip of one's fingers. In the early 1990s, only one in five households had a computer. Less than one percent of the population owned cellphones, and vehicle navigation systems were in the introductory stage. Internet access and email were not available until 1993. News about the road circulated almost entirely by way of publications, word of mouth, and personal correspondence.

Yet lack of information or exploratory tools discouraged almost no one. Most "roadies," as they came to be called, enjoyed touring the parts they could find, and many welcomed the challenge of searching them out. In 1994, the first edition of *Here It Is! The Route 66 Map Series* was published, providing turn-by-turn directions to keep tourists on track. It was another door opened. By now the route was generating its own energy, and the renaissance snowballed throughout the 1990s.

The first state-operated museum opened in Clinton, Oklahoma, in 1995.
Courtesy of Shellee Graham

In honor of the route's 70th anniversary, in 1996 antique dealers George and Melba Rook hosted the first national gathering of Route 66 aficionados under a tent next to their rural Landergin, Texas, store. In attendance were recognized advocates and hundreds of others from around the country. It would be the first in a succession of events hosted thereafter by the National Historic Route 66 Federation at various locations, further spreading the gospel of the route.

State associations sponsored annual cruises, and various cities began hosting their own festivals. By the mid-1990s, gift shops from Chicago to L.A. stocked Route 66 books, art, collectibles, and souvenirs, and online auctions offered thousands of items. The first local Route 66 museum had opened in McLean, Texas, in 1991. The state-operated Oklahoma Route 66 Museum was dedicated in 1995, followed three years later by the National Route 66 Museum in nearby Elk City. By the end of the decade, others dotted the map across all eight states. In 1999, the Route 66 Corridor Preservation Act, to be administered by the National Park Service, was passed by Congress, providing rehabilitation grants and a multitude of resources.

Documentaries were filmed, by both independent artists and national broadcasting companies. Preservationists got busy helping property owners refurbish their historic buildings, and efforts were undertaken to restrain highway departments from demolishing vintage bridges and original paving. Associations encouraged community leaders to capitalize on their Route 66 heritage and worked to promote tourism.

Murals like this one by Quarles Art in Tucumcari, New Mexico, are a growing part of the Route 66 experience. *Courtesy of Shellee Graham*

Route 66 ambassador Jerry McClanahan photographs the vintage Blue Swallow Motel in 2008. *Courtesy of Shellee Graham*

Renaissance fever inspired the owners of Carthage, Missouri's 66 Drive-In to convert its use as a salvage yard back to its intended purpose in 1998. *Courtesy of Jim Ross*

By the year 2000, several states had designated portions of the route as state highways. Tourist traffic had injected economic vitality into dozens of communities sorely in need. Historic route signs now marked much of the highway, and more businesses sought to benefit from their Mother Road heritage. Route 66 was in vogue, and advertisers latched on, combining popular culture and the promise of adventure with the magnetism of the highway.

The renaissance was further propelled in 2006 with the release of the Pixar film *Cars*, which delivered the single biggest publicity boost since the route's bureaucratic death. More than that, it

Historic Route 66 signs helped reestablish the former path of the Mother Road. *Courtesy of Shellee Graham*

German photographer Holger Hoetzel's 1992 book helped introduce the route to Europeans. *Authors' Collection*

Flo's V8 Cafe at Cars Land in Anaheim, California, 2013. *Courtesy of Shellee Graham*

introduced a younger generation to the wonders of the road, crucial to the highway's future. The subsequent development of Disney's Cars Land at their California theme park demonstrated confidence in the strength and permanence of the highway's pull.

Promotional efforts surged. States and towns began laying claim to having the biggest, the only, the longest, the tallest, the oldest, or some other Route 66 distinction. Illinois is "where the road begins," and Oklahoma has "more drivable miles of Route 66 than any state." Kansas has the shortest stretch of Mother Road at only 13 miles. Springfield, Missouri, bills itself as the "birthplace of Route 66," while Seligman, Arizona, is the birthplace of "Historic Route 66." Tulsa, home of Cyrus Avery, has proclaimed itself the "capital" of the route. The "longest" Route 66 urban boulevard is found in Albuquerque, while the route's "midpoint" is Adrian, Texas. In California, the Santa Monica pier is the symbolic "end of the trail."

The route was back, and well ahead of its centennial. Those expecting a saturation point by the 75th anniversary in 2001 came to realize that such a thing was not predictable. International tourists began to swamp the route, accounting for a significant percentage of visitors. They now have their own associations, generate global publicity, and contribute creatively. Innumerable Route 66 groups exist on social media platforms, some with memberships in the hundreds of thousands. Events, cruises, and conferences fill calendars.

Route 66 in its afterlife is very much a coin with two sides. One side reveals that as a national landmark and nostalgic playground, the road's future and popularity are assured. The flip side represents the keepers of the highway, those who live and work along its reaches and serve as hosts, helpers, advisors, and guides to all who encounter them. It is they who keep the motor running and the windshield wiped. It is the two sides combined that keep the magic of the Mother Road alive.

4 Women on the Route (now Cars on the Route) in Galena, Kansas, gained fame when the character Tow Mater from the Pixar film *Cars* was inspired by their vintage tow truck.
Courtesy of Jim Ross

Since 1935, the Wagon Wheel Motel in Cuba, Missouri, has been a Route 66 landmark.
Courtesy of Rhys Martin

Remains of the Two Guns, Arizona, tourist trap complex. *Courtesy of Jim Ross*

Roadside Attractions

ROADSIDE ATTRACTIONS during the highway's glory years were not in short supply. Those still operating now enjoy landmark status. Those that failed to survive but still exist in various states of ruin retain their appeal as well, sought out by those who want to behold ghosts of the road before they are gone. The same holds true for abandoned roadbed and bridges still clinging to the land.

Abandoned roadbed is a popular draw. With caution, the "Cuervo Cutoff" east of Santa Rosa, New Mexico, can still be explored. *Courtesy of Jim Ross*

The deteriorating Howdy Hanks at Joseph City, Arizona, harkens to the vacation boom years. *Courtesy of Shellee Graham*

A rare Luten Arch bridge built in 1914 and bypassed in 1937 still spans Canyon Padre east of Winona, Arizona. *Courtesy of Jim Ross*

The Snake Pit at the ruin of Clar's Hitching Post east of Moriarty, New Mexico, now haunts the service road to I-40. *Courtesy of Jim Ross*

Newer attractions staking their claim mix with the old. With budget and time constraints burdening fast-paced heritage tourists, competition remains strong for those out to make a buck. At the 100-year mark, joining the ranks of the old guard on the "must-see" list requires imagination and the kind of curb appeal that roadies cannot pass up. Photo albums enshrine road trips, so the bigger and more eye-catching the hook, the better.

These few examples only hint at what awaits the Route 66 explorer. Stir in some unexpected finds, a few ghost towns, and the comforting glow of neon at a vintage motor court. Season it with savory home cooking and a sack full of souvenirs, and the result will be a suitcase full of memories sure to inspire a return to the road.

The imposing 66-foot-tall pop bottle at POPS in Arcadia, Oklahoma, was raised in 2007. *Courtesy of Jim Ross*

The Blue Whale, seen here before being acquired by the City of Catoosa, Oklahoma, in 2020. It is now a city park. *Courtesy of Dean Kennedy*

San Bernardino's Wigwam Motel was restored under new ownership in the post-Route 66 era. *Courtesy of Shellee Graham*

The festive Santa Monica Pier is a candy-colored welcome to the western end of the route. *Courtesy of Carol Hightower, Library of Congress*

To the delight of tourists, wild burros roam the streets in Oatman, Arizona. *Courtesy of Don Schimmel*

The world's biggest rocking chair at Fanning, Missouri's Route 66 Outpost. *Courtesy of Jim Ross*

Tee-Pee Curios in Tucumcari has been a tourist magnet since its Native American façade was created in 1960. *Courtesy of Shellee Graham*

The Gay Parita station at Paris Springs, Missouri, built in 2006 by the late Gary Turner, is a tribute to an earlier station previously occupying the site. *Courtesy of Shellee Graham*

Winslow, Arizona, is home to the *Standin' on the Corner* statue. *Courtesy of Shellee Graham*

The General Store in Hackberry, Arizona, evolved as a tourist attraction in the 1990s under the ownership of the late Route 66 artist and ambassador Bob Waldmire, who inspired the character Fillmore in the Pixar film *Cars*. *Courtesy of Jim Ross*

Cadillac Ranch in Amarillo, Texas, has become one of the nation's most visited attractions. *Courtesy of Shellee Graham*

Painted Desert Trading Post, Arizona.
© *Robert Jensen*

CHAPTER 12

Preservation

EGLECT IMITATES RUST. Without intervention, it yields the same destructive effects as corrosion on steel. In time, a forsaken object collapses under its own weight. It doesn't require the wrath of nature or human effort. All it takes is a blind eye to its preservation.

Saving the route's valued sites requires a combined effort that often involves state historic preservation offices and other organizations. National Register of Historic Places listings, while helpful, actually offer little in the way of protection. The most successful projects almost always begin with a watchful eye at the grassroots level by those committed to keeping links to the past present and accounted for.

Some segments of the route have become historic byways or were granted state highway status, and its designation at the federal level as a National Historic Trail will have a long-term positive effect. But the bread and butter of preservation is saving individual properties. Aside from unavoidable losses due to fire, vandalism, and acts of God, such efforts most often take place on one of two fronts.

The first involves convincing owners to consider alternatives to demolition. Their reasons could involve insurance costs, safety concerns, desire to repurpose, or another legitimate issue. Preservationists must offer realistic options or find a way to assume ownership. Losses may be big or small, but each one weakens the road's historic integrity and dilutes the experience for travelers. Rescues, on the other hand, help sustain the route's appeal and preserve its heritage.

El Vado Motel in Albuquerque. *Courtesy of Rhys Martin*

The second front involves government agencies, particularly those holding sway over first-generation paving and historic bridges. Two of the route's most significant spans, both unique, were saved only after prolonged efforts. The Chain of Rocks Bridge on the Mississippi River, closed in 1968, narrowly escaped dismantling more than once. Today it is part of a managed hiking and biking trail. A 10-year battle to save the Gasconade River Bridge near Hazelgreen, Missouri, was waged from 2014 to 2024 and won. In each case, the outcome was the result of determination, perseverance, and public support. Still, losses far outnumber wins.

Tulsa's 66 Motel, lost in 2001. *Courtesy of Anthony Reichardt*

Gasconade River Bridge, Hazelgreen, Missouri. *Courtesy of Jim Ross*

Paving excavation east of Bridgeport, Oklahoma, 2000. *Courtesy of Jim Ross*

The Alvarado Hotel. *Authors' Collection*

Some worthy structures disappear almost unnoticed; others go down only after highly publicized efforts to save them fail, as in the case of the landmark Coral Court Motel in St. Louis. Whether a loss is obscure or high profile, each one affects the route's iconography. Occasionally, lessons learned serve as a wake-up call, as in the case of Albuquerque's Alvarado Hotel.

The Alvarado was the largest of the Harvey Houses, completed in 1902 in the Mission Revival style. Six decades later, it lingered in

Club Café in Santa Rosa, New Mexico, razed in 2014. *Courtesy of Shellee Graham*

Chain of Rocks Bridge, 1929. *Steve Rider Collection*

disrepair as one of the few Harvey hotels still standing. Owned by the Atchison, Topeka, and Santa Fe Railroad, it was offered to the city, but officials declined the $1.5 million asking price, and the hotel complex was destroyed in March 1970. Its removal is now considered the city's greatest architectural loss and prompted the creation of Albuquerque's conservation and historic landmarks programs. One state over, in 1997 preservationist and entrepreneur Allan Affeldt purchased and successfully restored the derelict and highly endangered La Posada Harvey House in Winslow, Arizona. Other surviving Harvey Houses on the route include La Fonda in Santa Fe, El Garces in Needles, California, and Casa del Desierto in Barstow. All have been preserved.

Icons either abandoned or in a state of ruin are susceptible to arson. Likewise, losses can occur from unintentional fire or an owner's death. Faulty electrical systems are often the culprit, as in the case of Clinton, Oklahoma's Pop Hicks restaurant, whose owners couldn't afford to replace old wiring and lost their insurance. Similarly, an owner's passing may mean the end of a property's existence. The Coliseum Ballroom and Miles Mahan's Hula Ville serve as examples of each.

Local grocer Dominic Tarro put

Alvarado demolition, 1970.
Albuquerque Museum, gift of Joe McKinney

Casa Del Desierto, Barstow, California.
Courtesy of Shellee Graham

Benld, Illinois, on the map when he built the Coliseum Ballroom there in 1924. Its 10,000-square-foot dance floor drew big-name acts and big crowds to this small community about an hour each direction from Springfield, Illinois, and St. Louis, Missouri. Benld is on IL 4, which initially served as US 66, and during Prohibition it became a hotspot notorious for boozing and gambling. In 1930, the year the route was moved, Dominic Tarro went missing following his indictment for collusion with bootleggers. Months later his waterlogged body was found in the Sangamon River in Springfield, purportedly the result of mob action. The Coliseum continued to thrive for decades, but eventually became an antique mall where musicians appeared only on weekends. On July 30, 2011, a performance by the band Shadow of Doubt was interrupted by an electrical fire that completely gutted the structure. The brick shell was later razed, leaving no trace of the landmark building.

Not a great deal is known about Miles Mahan, creator of the Hula Ville folk-art garden that featured displays of his hand-lettered poetry and a disjointed collection of scavenged signs. Mahan spent his career as a carny before retiring in 1956 to a small tract of sandy turf in the California desert near Hesperia. There, he crafted kitschy

Coliseum Ballroom in 2010.
Courtesy of Karas A. Hall

Fire damage at the Coliseum.
Courtesy of Jim Marcacci

Hula Ville signs in Hesperia, California. *Courtesy of Shellee Graham*

Miles Mahan at Hula Ville. *Courtesy of Shellee Graham*

Roadrunner Lodge, Tucumcari, New Mexico. *Courtesy of KC Keefer*

sculptures, played golf on a three-hole course of his own design, and composed poems, many of them based on colorful carnival people from his past. Commercial signs he pulled from dumps added to the brew, including a hula girl that became the property's namesake. Hula Ville evolved as a tourist attraction, and in 1981 it became a California Historical Landmark. In spite of its declared significance, when Mahan passed in 1997, the orphaned Hula Ville reverted to the barren patch of earth he had started with, but not before many of his creations were recovered and placed on display at Victorville's California Route 66 Museum.

A vacant structure may be spared for years simply because there is little demand for the ground holding it up or no dollars available for taking it down. With luck, the more appealing among them manage to hang on until the right person or organization brings them back to life. Those who buy and rehabilitate these derelict treasures are a special breed. To drop anchor and gamble everything takes more than an attraction to the route's popularity and mystique. It requires a belief in the intrinsic value and potential of the site as well as a willingness to take enormous risk. Not all succeed, but those who do

Cool Springs Camp, Arizona.
Courtesy of Jim Ross

Shamrock Court during renovation.
Courtesy of Shellee Graham

encourage more of the same. Shining successes include Tucumcari's Motel Safari and Roadrunner Lodge, Arizona's Cool Springs Camp, and the Shamrock Court in Sullivan, Missouri.

The Boots Court in Carthage, Missouri, built by Arthur Boots in 1939, is another prominent rescue. The Streamline Moderne–style motel featured eight units under a flat roof with covered parking spaces separating the rooms. Boots sold it to the Neeley family, who added a five-room wing behind the original building in 1946. Ownership over the years continued to change until decline set in. In the early 2000s, then-owner Johnnie Ferguson sold it to a developer, but public outcry prevented its destruction, and for several years it was used for short-term rentals. In 2011, the Boots

The fully restored Boots Motel in Carthage, Missouri, now offers an authentic retro experience. *Courtesy of Shellee Graham*

was acquired by a local bank, which then sold it to preservationist sisters Debye Harvey and Priscilla Bledsaw. They removed a gabled roof added in the 1970s, renovated most of the rooms, got it listed on the National Register, and successfully reopened it as a motel. After eight years, they sold it to two local couples, who set up a nonprofit foundation and completed the restoration, including exterior refurbishment.

In the late 1980s, when Arcadia, Oklahoma's Round Barn was donated to the newly formed Arcadia Historical and Preservation Society (AHPS), it was almost beyond salvation. Even so, with

The state of the Round Barn in 1988. *Courtesy of Maxine Campbell*

the Route 66 revival getting underway, Arcadia stood to gain handsomely if it could be saved. Rancher William Odor had raised the barn in 1898, using milled strips of green burr oak soaked in the nearby Deep Fork River to make them bend. The imposing barn was 60 feet in diameter, and its domed roof peaked at 43 feet above the ground. Carpenters convinced Odor to use hardwood flooring in the loft for hosting dances, and when finished the barn became a prime spot for socializing. Ninety years later, with the roof collapsed and the walls buckling, the AHPS and a crew of seniors led by retired master carpenter Luke Robison began a monumental attempt at resurrection. Media attention led to donations of greenbacks, materials, and equipment, and in 1992 the project was completed. Now one of the most visited landmarks on the route, a gift shop and museum occupy the barn's ground floor, while the loft's vintage hardwood floors are once again used for boot-scootin' and special events.

The Round Barn's loft is now used for special events.
Courtesy of Shellee Graham

The U-Drop Inn and Tower Station in Shamrock, Texas, was built by John Nunn in 1936. Nunn had simply sketched his vision for the building in the dirt, and architect Joseph Champ Berry and builders J. M. Tindall and R. C. Lewis took it from there. When finished, the massive, neon-trimmed art-deco edifice stood tall on the Texas prairie, dominating

U-Drop Inn and Tower Station in Shamrock, Texas.
Courtesy of Keith George

Round Barn in 2021.
Courtesy of Shellee Graham

the landscape for miles. Nunn leased the station, while he and his wife, Bebe, managed the café. After their retirement, the complex changed hands numerous times until it became vacant. In 1999 it was purchased by a local bank and gifted to the city after various attempts at adaptive reuse failed. Following discussions regarding its future, a Dallas-based preservation group was retained, which led to a $1.7 million restoration grant from the Transportation Equity Act for the 21st Century. Work was completed in 2003. Fuel is no longer pumped there, but the café reopened, and a welcome center and gift shop now occupy connecting space. At the grand opening event, cheers rang out when a flipped switch once again cast the colorful glow of neon into the vast Texas night.

Going forward, increased awareness will help balance the ratio of losses to saves, but it will require sustained effort. In the wake of the interstate cyclone, most small towns became skeletons of what they had been, and maintaining economic viability continues to leave little in the resource cupboard for saving endangered sites. Praiseworthy are the town leaders, preservationists, grant providers, donors, organizations, and investors who still find a way to make it happen.

Sprague's Super Service, Normal, Illinois. *Courtesy of Rich Dinkela*

Standard Station in Odell, Illinois. *Courtesy of Jim Ross*

CASE STUDY

The Painted Desert Trading Post

QUINTING AGAINST the Arizona sun, Dotch Windsor worked his cattle from horseback, but his attention was drawn to the motorists streaming by his small ranch fronting US 66. Dotch had come to Arizona from New Mexico in the late 1930s, settling on a patch of desert next to the Dead River and just east of the Painted Desert. He determined, rightly, that there was money to be made from tourists, and around 1940 he opened the Painted Desert Trading Post on his highway frontage. Business was steady for nearly 20 years, but in 1958 the route was relocated and he was left stranded on an abandoned stretch of roadway. Dotch packed up and moved to Holbrook, where he died six years later. The deserted trading post was never reopened or repurposed. Except for whistling wind and the howls of song dogs, silence shrouded the site for the next six decades.

By the 1990s, the trading post had become a crown jewel among Route 66 icons, its isolation and originality appealing to the more seasoned roadies, who ventured down a long, dead-end stretch of fractured asphalt to reach it. The property had passed through various hands over the years, but the trading post remained

The only known postcard of the Painted Desert Trading Post, from 1945. *Mike Ward Collection*

The trading post as it appeared when nearing collapse in 2018. *Courtesy of Terry Drewitz*

uncared for and deteriorating. By 2015 it was so distressed that preservationists contacted the absentee owner for permission to stabilize it, but promises made were not kept.

Three years later, as collapse of the building appeared imminent, it was listed for sale. Roadie Rich Dinkela of Missouri heard about it and straightaway rounded up a group of eight other like-minded enthusiasts willing to ante up hard-earned dollars and get their hands dirty. They hurriedly formed the nonprofit Route 66 Co-Op and purchased the building and surrounding 94 acres.

A detailed inspection revealed that a half-century of water and wind erosion had caused the foundation to fail and the roof to rot. Cattle had heavily damaged the exterior stucco. Walls sagged and bulged. One corner of the building rested on the ground 16 inches below the concrete slab floor. Ravens and rodents were permanent residents.

The Co-Op applied for a National Park Service grant and received generous donations from supporters, both domestic and international. Coaching from restoration experts connected to similar projects helped them devise a three-phase rescue plan that would lift and straighten the walls, replace the roof structure, and install a new foundation. Bulk materials and rental equipment were trailered 60 miles from Gallup, New Mexico. Water was hauled in,

The severely slumped southeast corner of the building is lifted using multiple jack posts. *Courtesy of Shellee Graham*

The roof of the trading post had to be completely removed and rebuilt.
Courtesy of Rich Dinkela

and a generator powered saws and drills. Using Holbrook, Arizona, as a base of operations, one-week work sessions took place in the spring and fall, drawing volunteers from all over the country.

Among the Co-Op members, three had backgrounds in construction management. Other members and volunteers included a physicist, two professional engineers, roofers, carpenters, a heavy-equipment operator, and one journeyman concrete finisher. Skill sets were varied enough that no outside contractors were required, saving considerable expense.

Raising the walls began with the corners, where timber beams were bolted against the ceiling joists on the inside. Four-by-four timber jack-posts were then placed under the beams, their bottoms resting on five-ton screw jacks. The multiple jacks were then slowly and simultaneously turned until the bottom sill plates were raised to floor level. Temporary "shear" walls were then constructed 18 inches inside and parallel to the existing exterior walls to hold them in their restored positions. This allowed the jacks to be moved and the process repeated around the perimeter of the building.

With the walls repositioned and stabilized, the entire roof structure was removed and replaced, incorporating as many original ceiling joists, rafters, and braces as possible. Roof decking to match the original was milled at a specialty shop in Albuquerque, and new but matching galvanized steel roofing panels were installed. Parapet walls were capped with custom-made flashing, and sealant was used to ensure a watertight roof.

Because of unpredictable high winds, beams were extended through window and door openings for additional support, and a trench was then dug beneath the building's exterior walls. With the trading post fully levitated, the bottoms of wall studs were trimmed and new sill plates attached to match the level of the slab floor. Reinforcing steel bars were positioned in the completed trough and plywood forms built. Concrete, trucked from 50 miles

Preparation for the new foundation required levitation of the entire buidling.
Courtesy of Jim Ross

The trading post remains a non-operational relic but is no longer endangered. © *Robert Jensen*

The rescue's final phase consisted of stucco repair, painting, and lettering. *Courtesy of Steve Rider*

away in Joseph City, filled the encased perimeter trench up to the bottoms of the new sill plates, where J-bolts were used to anchor them to the concrete.

With the three-phase plan completed, sheathing and stucco were repaired, the building's exterior was painted, and "ghosted" lettering was applied to match the original. Inside, missing partitions were rebuilt and interpretive panels installed. In the fall of 2021, after three years, the trading post was ready for visitors. Gated access to the old roadway allowed for controlled entry.

By intent, the Painted Desert Trading Post remains a relic. It stands as it has since its abandonment, to be experienced one-on-one in the quiet of the desert, interrupted only by occasional gusts of wind or the caws of wandering ravens. It is efforts like this one, driven by a passion to preserve what came before for those who will come later, that help sustain the legend of the Mother Road.

EPILOGUE

The Next 100 Years

SKEPTICS SAY the route is overhyped, over commercialized, and overrated. They declare that Route 66 was supplanted by the interstates and that whatever importance it once held is gone. One graduate school student wrote a thesis attempting to equate the route's legend with fictionalized 19th century dime novels. A common thread among these naysayers is that their approach seems to carry with it an expectation of disappointment. Rarely do they move beyond the surface.

While the interstates hijacked a number of segments, almost all of the route survives, as do the communities, landmarks, quirky attractions, and haunts, all of them woven into a linear museum stretched across eight states. Vintage motels continue to host tourists, and diners like Robert's Grill in El Reno, Oklahoma, still serve up juicy burgers, as they have since 1926. You can sleep in a wigwam, prowl the ruins at Two Guns, behold Meteor Crater, collect roadside totems, and spend hours cruising two-lane pavement stitched to the lay of the land, having it mostly to yourself. Waiting around every curve is a new chance for discovery.

The reverence held for the route in popular culture is justified and genuine, its legend undeniable. As geographer Arthur Krim points out, "Like the Mississippi of Mark Twain, US 66 was a river of migration and opportunity to the western frontier." The nearly immediate launching of the renaissance following its premature demise was destined. During the four decades since, the keepers of the highway have welcomed and befriended new generations of road warriors, nourishing and building upon all that has come before.

Dog on 66, Afton, Oklahoma, 1993.
Courtesy of Shellee Graham

The future of the route is not in doubt. One hundred years from now its value as an American treasure will be stronger than today. More communities are coming on board, capitalizing on its popularity and curating their own icons. Route 66 is now embedded in state tourism efforts, and highway builders better understand the need to preserve original roadbed and integral structures. Internationally, the route is regarded as the world's most famous highway, and it should be. Tourists from around the globe find their way along its reaches by the thousands each year, drawn not only by the lore of the highway, but by the vast expanse of the American West and a chance for adventure in the land of the free. More will join them.

Here's to the next 100 years. And beyond.

Courtesy of Sue Ann (Miller) Dunn and Charles Miller

Boy perched on Arizona highway sign. *66postcards.com*

State line sign at Glenrio, New Mexico. *Authors' Collection*

66postcards.com

Cynthia Troup poses next to a New Mexico sign. *Courtesy of the Troup Family Archives*

Happy Trails

In the pre-interstate days, travelers made the journey part of the destination by collecting souvenir spoons, matchbooks, window decals, postcards, bumper stickers, brochures, and even roadside totems found along the way. Such mementos fostered a sense of bonding with the open road. Plenty of photos were taken as well, and a popular subject was the ever-reliable highway sign.

Courtesy of Tim Wisinger

Bill McDermott (right) and friend with Missouri sign post in 1943. Bill was stationed at nearby Camp Crowder. *Courtesy of Alice McDermott*

Twin sisters strike a pose in Pontiac, Illinois, circa 1950s. *66postcards.com*

Authors' Collection

Author Jack Rittenhouse next to a California US 66 shield. *© HBLT, used with permission from the Harry Briley Living Trust.*

Blue Swallow Motel owner Lillian Redman in Arizona. *Courtesy of the Blue Swallow Motel.*

Color-coded road signs in Flagstaff, Arizona, 1950s. *66postcards.com*

Along the Oklahoma City beltline route, 1940s. *Authors' Collection*

At the Colorado River, circa 1940s. *Courtesy of Mike Hede*

Making memories in Edwardsville, Illinois. *66postcards.com*

Entering California from Arizona, circa 1940s. *66postcards.com*

Road Facts

November 11, 1926, is the benchmark date for the route's birth, but each state had to formally approve the new federal highways, which occurred at different times over a period of weeks.

Changes to the route have been ongoing since it was designated. Its overall length can only be calculated using a given point in time. A ballpark figure is 2,450 miles.

In the beginning, the route's turn-by-turn pathway was not precisely defined. Because of this, its exact length at inception is not known.

The route was entirely paved to uniform standards by 1938.

Originally, New Mexico had the most miles of Route 66. When the loop through Santa Fe was removed in 1937, Oklahoma became the state with the most miles.

Interstate construction consumed more of the route in Arizona than in any other state.

The Oklahoma State Capitol, the original Illinois State Capitol, and the New Mexico State Capitol (during the era of US 66 through Santa Fe) were all on the route.

A common misunderstanding is that US 66 passed through Picher, Oklahoma. It didn't. Another is that the Ozark Trails obelisk west of Stroud, Oklahoma, was moved to that location from town. It wasn't.

Five different bridges have carried Route 66 traffic across the Mississippi River at St. Louis: the McKinley, Municipal-MacArthur, Chain

This WPA-built pedestrian underpass is on the route in El Reno, Oklahoma. *Courtesy of Jim Ross*

of Rocks, Veterans-MLK, and Poplar Street Bridge, in that order.

The symbolic western terminus of US 66 is the Santa Monica Pier. The original terminus is the intersection of 7th and Broadway in downtown L.A. This was moved in the 1930s to Lincoln and Olympic Boulevards in Santa Monica.

California was the last state to mark US 66 with highway shields, well over a year after the route's official designation.

In 1983, the Route 66 resort community of Times Beach, Missouri, was condemned, razed, and the land there quarantined for 14 years due to contamination from toxic chemicals applied to its unpaved streets. It is now a state park.

During the years US 66 passed through the hearts of towns, pedestrian underpasses (subways) were common near schools, churches, and busy intersections. A handful (some in use) are still in place.

In 1954, proposed plans for a four-lane expansion in the Oklahoma City metro included an elevated or subterranean roadway through the suburb of Bethany to avoid multiple intersections. It was never built.

A Federal Aid Project boundary marker near Arcadia, Oklahoma. *Courtesy of Jim Ross*

In addition to the mainline US 66, other designations included Temporary, Business, City, Truck, Bypass, Alternate, and Beltline routes. Only St. Louis, Missouri, and Venice, Illinois, had an alignment designated "Optional."

A 16-mile stretch of one-lane paving (nine feet wide) carried US 66 traffic between Miami and Afton, Oklahoma, until its 1937 bypass. Six miles of the "Sidewalk Highway" survives in two sections.

Road Facts

Oklahoma and Texas were the only Route 66 states to install concrete Federal Aid Project markers with embedded brass shields identifying road project boundaries. Very few remain.

As the interstates were built, a requirement that one mile in every five be level and contain no curves to accommodate military aircraft is a myth.

In places, US 66 was constructed on former railroad beds.

A section of first-generation concrete paving harvested in western Oklahoma is now part of the "America on the Move" exhibition at the Smithsonian's National Museum of American History.

The highest elevation on the route is near Parks, Arizona, at just over 7,300 feet. The lowest elevation is in Santa Monica, California, at 105 feet.

When construction began in 1941, the rock cut through Hooker Ridge at Hooker, Missouri, was the deepest in the country at 93 feet.

In places, US 66 adopted former railroad beds. This one is near Los Lunas, New Mexico. *Courtesy of Jim Ross*

First generation concrete paving destined for the Smithsonian Institution, 1999.
Oklahoma Department of Transportation

Albuquerque's 4th Street and Central Avenue is known as the intersection where the original alignment and its replacement alignment cross each other, but such crossings occur elsewhere on the route.

Not all official highway shields were made of metal. A limited number were constructed of wood.

In McCook, Illinois, a one-mile section of the route has been permanently closed due to the destabilizing effects of quarry operations on both sides of the roadway.

In Missouri and Oklahoma, sections of first-generation paving built with sloped curbs survive and remain in use. Their purpose was to keep water on the roadway to preserve soft shoulders.

The longest uninterrupted stretch of surviving Route 66 (without involving large cities) is from I-40 Exit 139 west of Ash Fork, Arizona, to just west of the Holy Moses Wash Bridge west of Kingman, Arizona, a distance of 108 miles.

Standard-issue US highway shields did not contain the word ROUTE.

Route 66: The First 100 Years Timeline

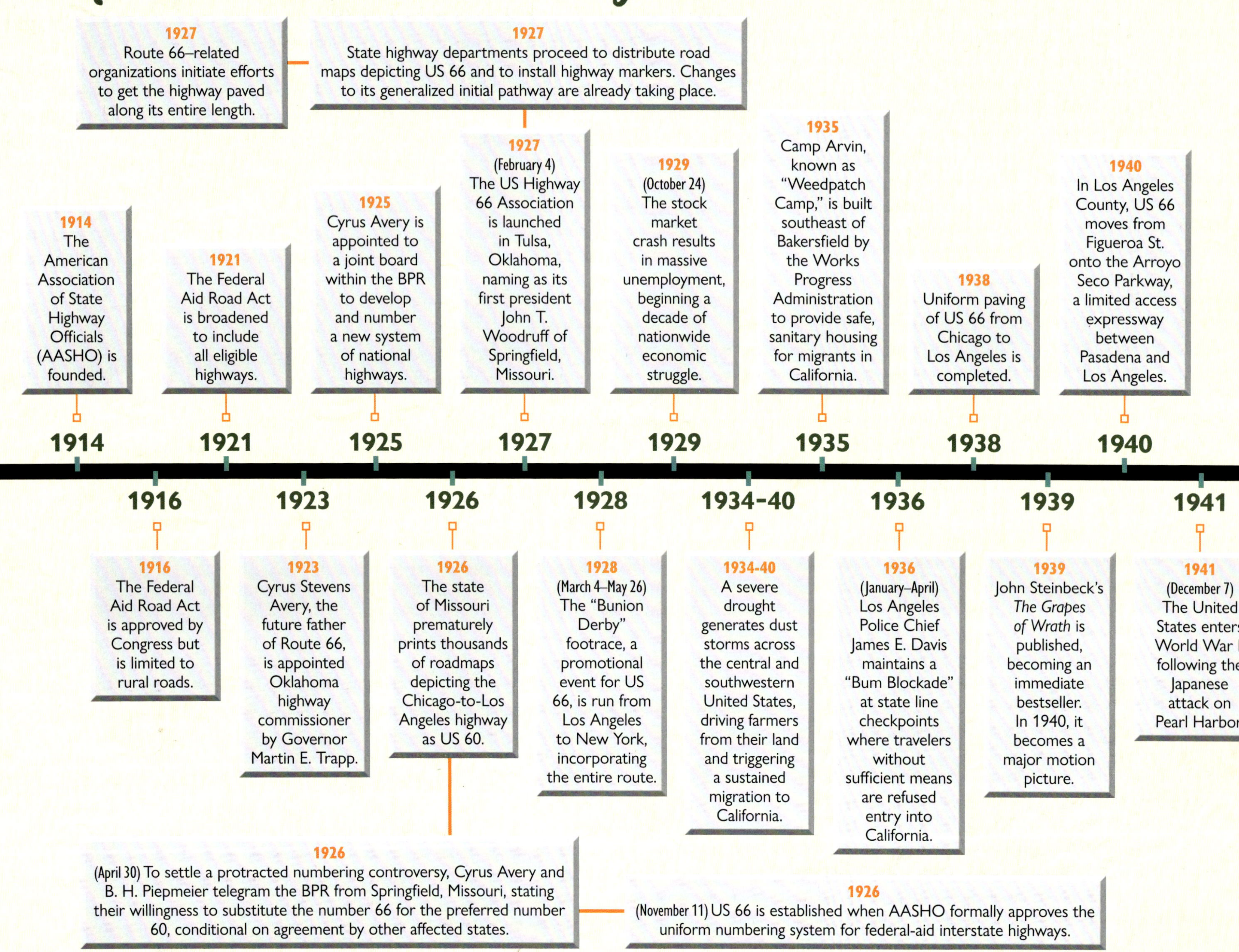

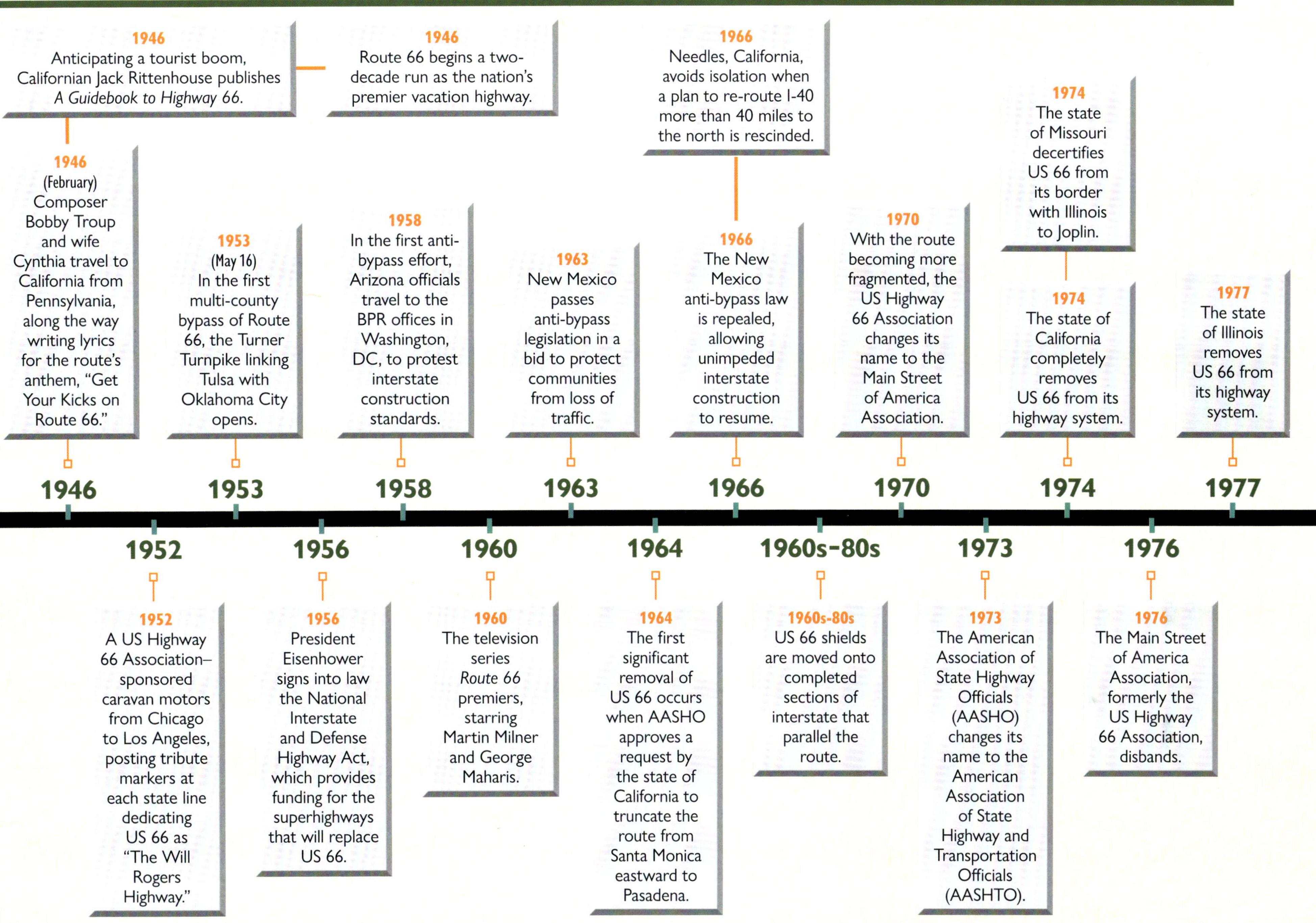

1946 Anticipating a tourist boom, Californian Jack Rittenhouse publishes *A Guidebook to Highway 66*.
1946 Route 66 begins a two-decade run as the nation's premier vacation highway.
1946 (February) Composer Bobby Troup and wife Cynthia travel to California from Pennsylvania, along the way writing lyrics for the route's anthem, "Get Your Kicks on Route 66."
1952 A US Highway 66 Association–sponsored caravan motors from Chicago to Los Angeles, posting tribute markers at each state line dedicating US 66 as "The Will Rogers Highway."
1953 (May 16) In the first multi-county bypass of Route 66, the Turner Turnpike linking Tulsa with Oklahoma City opens.
1956 President Eisenhower signs into law the National Interstate and Defense Highway Act, which provides funding for the superhighways that will replace US 66.
1958 In the first anti-bypass effort, Arizona officials travel to the BPR offices in Washington, DC, to protest interstate construction standards.
1960 The television series *Route 66* premieres, starring Martin Milner and George Maharis.
1963 New Mexico passes anti-bypass legislation in a bid to protect communities from loss of traffic.
1964 The first significant removal of US 66 occurs when AASHO approves a request by the state of California to truncate the route from Santa Monica eastward to Pasadena.
1966 Needles, California, avoids isolation when a plan to re-route I-40 more than 40 miles to the north is rescinded.
1966 The New Mexico anti-bypass law is repealed, allowing unimpeded interstate construction to resume.
1960s–80s US 66 shields are moved onto completed sections of interstate that parallel the route.
1970 With the route becoming more fragmented, the US Highway 66 Association changes its name to the Main Street of America Association.
1973 The American Association of State Highway Officials (AASHO) changes its name to the American Association of State Highway and Transportation Officials (AASHTO).
1974 The state of Missouri decertifies US 66 from its border with Illinois to Joplin.
1974 The state of California completely removes US 66 from its highway system.
1976 The Main Street of America Association, formerly the US Highway 66 Association, disbands.
1977 The state of Illinois removes US 66 from its highway system.

Pontiac at Blue Swallow Motel,
Tucumcari, New Mexico.
Courtesy of Shellee Graham

1984 (October 8) Williams, Arizona, becomes the last city to be bypassed by an interstate.

1985 (April) The state of Oklahoma removes US 66 from its highway system.

1985 (June) AASHTO removes all remaining designations of US 66.

1987 The first Historic Route 66 Association is organized in Seligman, Arizona.

1990 Congress approves the Route 66 Study Act to explore alternatives for its preservation.

1990 The publication of *Route 66: The Mother Road* by author Michael Wallis fuels renewed national interest in the route.

1991 Route 66 associations now exist in all eight states.

1992 Celebrations are held to commemorate the route's 66th anniversary.

1993 *Route 66 Magazine* debuts, beginning a 28-year run.

1994 The National Historic Route 66 Federation is founded, with a focus on preserving the route.

1995 Filmmaker John Paget releases *Route 66: An American Odyssey*, a feature-length, independently produced documentary.

1996 Run to the Heartland, the first Route 66 gathering national in scope, is held in Landergin, Texas

1999 The Route 66 Corridor Preservation Program is approved by Congress.

2001 (November 11) Route 66 celebrates its 75th anniversary.

2021 H.R. 3600 is introduced in Congress to designate Route 66 a National Historic Trail.

2026 (November 11) Route 66 celebrates its 100th anniversary.

Courtesy of Jim Ross

Route 66 in Williams, Arizona, was populated with neon signs by the late 1930s. View is east from Third Street.
66 postcards.com

Don't miss the 13 miles of Kansas 66.
Courtesy of Renee Charles and Cheron Myers

Courtesy of Shellee Graham

Authors' Collection

Bar-Len Drive-In Theater, 1994,
Lenwood, California.
Courtesy of Jim Ross

Footnotes

Chapter 1: * "From Names to Numbers," Richard F. Weingroff, AASHTO Quarterly, Spring 1997.
** *Ibid.*

Chapter 4: * "The Bum Blockade: Los Angeles and the Great Depression," Giczy, Hailey, Voces Novae: Vol. 1, Article 6 (2018), Chapman University.
** *Ibid.*

Sources

GENERAL

Authors' archives and collections.

Richard F. Weingroff, historian, Federal Highway Administration. Documents, articles, and correspondence pertaining to the evolution of the US highway system.

Detroit Historical Society

Northern Arizona University

American Association of State Highway and Transportation Officials

National Archives

Find a Grave®

Ancestry.com

US Census Bureau

Newspapers.com

Smithsonian Institute, Online Virtual Archives

Missouri State University Libraries

Missouri State Archives

Kansas Historical Society

Departments of Transportation in Illinois, Missouri, Kansas, Oklahoma, Texas, New Mexico, Arizona, and California

Oklahoma History Center

Mohave Historical Society

National Park Service

Library of Congress

Arcadia Historical and Preservation Society, Arcadia, Oklahoma

The Portal to Texas History: texashistory.unt.edu/search/

BOOKS / PAPERS / ARTICLES / DOCUMENTS

Coward, David E. *The Uncle We Never Knew: The Life of Elton Wayne Cooke (1919–1943)*, David R. Coward, 2012.

Federal Aid Highway Act of 1966. Committee on Public Works, Subcommittee on Roads, United States Senate.

Fried, Stephen. *Appetite for America*, Random House, 2010.

Graham, Shellee. *Tales from the Coral Court*, Virginia Publishing, 2000.

Kastner, Charles B. *Bunion Derby: The 1928 Footrace Across America*, University of New Mexico Press, 2007.

Kelley, Shawn, and Reynolds, Kristen. *Route 66 & Native Americans in New Mexico*, New Mexico Department of Transportation and Federal Highway Study, 2009.

Krim, Arthur. "Route 66: Auto River of the American West," *Geographical Snapshots of North America*, ed. Donald G. Janelle (New York: Guilford Press, 1992), p. 32.

Krim, Arthur. *Route 66: Iconography of the American Highway*, Center for American Places, 2006.

Lawler, Nan Marie. *The Ozark Trails Association*, a thesis submitted in partial fulfillment of the requirements for the degree of Master of Arts, University of Arkansas, 1991.

Marmon, Lee, and Corbett, Tom. *Laguna Pueblo, A Photographic History*, University of New Mexico Press, 2015.

McClanahan, Jerry; Ross, Jim; and Graham, Shellee. *Route 66 Sightings*, Ghost Town Press, 2011.

McConal, Patrick M. *Over the Wall: The Men Behind the 1934 Death House Escape*, Eakin Press, 2000.

O'Reilly, Kelly R. *Oklatopia: The Cultural Mission of California's Migratory Labor Camps, 1935–1941*, Senior Thesis, Department of History, Columbia University, 2012.

Rittenhouse, Jack. *A Guidebook to Highway 66*, self-published, 1946.

Rooker, Oliver. *Riding the Travel Bureau: Ghost Riders Network on Route 66 During the Great Depression*, Memoir Publishing, 1994.

Ross, Jim. *Oklahoma Route 66*, Ghost Town Press, 2011.

Ross, Jim. "Proud of What It Means" (cover story), *The Chronicles of Oklahoma*, Vol. LXXIII, Number Three, Fall 1995.

Ross, Jim. *Route 66 Crossings: Historic Bridges of the Mother Road*, University of Oklahoma Press, 2016.

Ross, Jim, and Graham, Shellee. *Secret Route 66: A Guide to the Weird, Wonderful, and Obscure*, Reedy Press, 2017.

Slaney, Deborah C. *Jewel of the Railroad Era: Albuquerque's Alvarado Hotel*, The Albuquerque Museum, 2009.

Steinbeck, John. *The Harvest Gypsies—On the Road to the Grapes of Wrath*, a reprint of articles from the *San Francisco News* in 1936, introduction by Charles Wollenberg, Heyday Books, 1988.

Wallis, Michael. *Route 66: The Mother Road*, St. Martin's Press, 1990.

Index

Oatman Road, Arizona.
Courtesy of Jim Ross